IMAGES
of America

KING RECORDS
OF CINCINNATI

In this 1993 photograph, the former King Records factory resembles a part of a Gothic film set. At that time, community leaders attempted—unsuccessfully—to erect a historical marker and turn the warehouse into a museum. James Brown wept when he saw it for the first time in decades. (Author's collection.)

On the cover: Taken around 1948, this image shows what King Records was all about—integrating races, sexes, and sounds. The unidentified employees sort 78-rpm discs to be sent to disc jockeys and record stores across the nation. (Courtesy of Steven D. Halper.)

IMAGES
of America

KING RECORDS
OF CINCINNATI

Randy McNutt

ARCADIA
PUBLISHING

Published by Arcadia Publishing
Charleston, South Carolina

Library of Congress Control Number: 2008940654

For all general information contact Arcadia Publishing at:
Telephone 843-853-2070
Fax 843-853-0044
E-mail sales@arcadiapublishing.com
For customer service and orders:
Toll-Free 1-888-313-2665

Visit us on the Internet at www.arcadiapublishing.com

Dedicated to my friends Bonnie Lou Okum and Rusty York—talented entertainers who have lived and performed with dignity, class, and cheerfulness. Through their work, they have made the world a little brighter. (Courtesy of Rusty York.)

CONTENTS

ACKNOWLEDGMENTS

Many generous people contributed their time, ideas, information, and illustrations to this project. If I have inadvertently omitted a few of their names, the oversight was unintentional.

First, I thank my old friends Rusty York and Bonnie Lou Okum, to whom this book is dedicated. Both are talented performers and pleasant people whose company I have enjoyed for years. I thank them for their patience and continued assistance.

Two other contributors were equally generous—Zella Nathan, wife of founder Sydney Nathan, and Steven D. Halper, Sydney's nephew and the son of founding co-investors Saul and Dorothy Halper. Without their help and encouragement, I could not have started the book. They opened their homes and scrapbooks to me, and I deeply appreciate their trust and generosity.

I also thank librarian Brian Powers and musician Elliot Ruther for their efforts to restore King's luster. Brian's own research is important, and throughout this project I have appreciated his enthusiasm, good humor, and advice. Elliot has helped organize events that have placed King Records back in the news, and he continues to promote Cincinnati's important place in the nation's musical history.

As usual, my deep appreciation and thanks go to my wife and line editor, Cheryl Bauer, for her expert eye, and to Melissa Basilone and John Pearson, my Arcadia Publishing editor and publisher, respectively. All three made the job a pleasure.

Others who helped include Lee Hay of WVXU Radio, Frank Weimann, Steve Lake, Darren Blase, Rick Kennedy, Toby Aydelott, Bob Snyder, Fred Masotti, Charles Spurling, Carl Edmondson, Bob Armstrong, Mike Banks, Shad O'Shea, Donna Newman, Deborah Delmore, Dick Swaim, Steve Rosen, David Meyers, and Liz Dufour and Ron Wild, my former colleagues at the *Cincinnati Enquirer.*

Finally, I am indebted to Annette Meurer and Barbara Hudson of Joseph-Beth Booksellers for their continued support of my books—and those of so many other writers.

INTRODUCTION

When Sydney Nathan founded Cincinnati's King Records in 1943, he acted out of frustration as much as ambition. For years he had struggled financially, operating a shooting gallery, promoting wrestling matches, and working in a radio store.

He had always wanted to leave his mark. Music—his own—afforded him the opportunity.

From his record shop on Central Avenue, Nathan sold his early King releases as well as many issued by the major labels. He did not have to look far to find his first recording artists. He simply turned on his radio and heard Grandpa Jones and Merle Travis, who worked as country staff musicians at powerful WLW Radio. Nathan met the Delmore Brothers, also station musicians, when they bought records from him.

In only four years, Nathan went from record shop owner to music industry innovator, doing nearly everything under one roof. At the end of World War II in 1945, King Records seriously started pressing records in its own factory at 1540 Brewster Avenue in the Evanston neighborhood. King's first pressing, a 78-rpm disc called "Filipino Baby" by Lloyd "Cowboy" Copas, became a national hit. Nathan bought more presses and expanded the plant. His records flew onto the charts.

In 1947, he finally built a recording studio in back of the loading dock; unfortunately, it was on property that King Records did not own at the time. "We had to scramble to make it right," recalled Howard Kessel, a company partner. Meanwhile, King continued to turn out national hits. Wisely Nathan sought singers who could write their own songs for the company's Lois Music. He experimented with their songs, mixing styles, genres, and musicians. He recorded pop songs with black and country singers, and country songs with pop singers. He refined the concept of the studio session band by hiring talented country musicians, including Zeke Turner on electric lead guitar; Louis Innis, bass and rhythm guitar; Kenneth "Jethro" Burns (of the duo Homer and Jethro), mandolin; Jerry Byrd, steel guitar; Tommy Jackson, fiddle; Wayne Raney, harmonica; Shorty Long, piano; and other guitarists such as Henry "Homer" Haynes, Billy Grammer, and Hank Garland. They were the best pickers of their day.

Determined to conduct nearly all King Records business on Brewster Avenue, Nathan set up machinery to press records, design album covers, master discs, and record the vocalists. In fact, King Records could do everything but make its own sleeves and shipping cartons, which were manufactured in Miamisburg, Ohio, about 45 miles north of Cincinnati.

Nathan's business acumen and keen ear for talent boosted King Records' reputation. In early 1947, *Billboard* magazine named the firm one of America's six leading record companies. Its acts ranged from black big band leader Lucky Millinder and sax man and singer "Bull Moose" Jackson to hillbilly singers "Hawkshaw" Hawkins and Hank Penny. Major black doo-wop and other vocal groups, including the Platters and the Swallows, recorded for King Records. So did a number of instrumentalists, including now under-appreciated sax men such as "Big Jay" McNeely, Sil Austin, and Tab Smith.

King Records also set trends inside the office, hiring significant numbers of minorities and women in an era when many companies would not. Nathan also allowed a union to represent his factory employees.

When country music went into a temporary decline in the mid-1950s, King Records depended more on its rhythm and blues acts. Some of them recorded so-called dirty songs such as "Sixty-Minute Man" by the Dominoes and "Annie Had a Baby" by the Royals. As King Records was poised to strike at the pop charts in 1955, however, it rejected what John S. Kelley Jr., a King Records vice president, called "double-entendre tunes." He admitted to *Variety* that the company was not without guilt but assured it would "never again allow off-color lyrics."

As King Records continued to grow, it retained its original ownership, a small group of friends and family that had originally backed Nathan. Investors included Howard Kessel, Nathan's second cousin and chief of Royal Plastics, the company's pressing division; and Dorothy Halper, Nathan's sister and owner-operator of a downtown record shop with her husband, Saul.

Unlike many record companies, King Records was happy to make regional sounds and promote local performers as well as national ones. One reason for this was King Records' self-contained factory and Nathan's pride and interest in the city. He felt connected. If he wanted to press only 500 copies of a long-shot single for a local singer, he could do it. And he did—many times, especially after the company began to manufacture large quantities of vinyl 45-rpm discs in the early 1950s. Nathan's local philosophy continued into the 1960s. Hometown acts included radio and television singers Bonnie Lou, Ruby Wright, the Hometowners, and Bob Braun. King Records also forged associations with local radio and television icons Ruth Lyons, Bob Shreve, and Waite Hoyt.

But King Records' real legacy is American roots music—jazz, country, bluegrass, polka, rockabilly, and the blues. From the bluegrass Stanley Brothers to R&B shouters James Brown and Hank Ballard, the company helped establish the careers of hundreds of struggling performers at a time when African Americans and Appalachians found it difficult to obtain recording contracts with major labels. King Records' varied artists went on to influence performers in all musical genres, but especially in jazz, country, blues, and R&B.

Distinctive in their ways and sounds, many King Records artists used odd nicknames that must have sounded funny to Cincinnati's mainstream pop radio listeners if they tuned in to shows like Nelson King's country music *Jamboree* on WCKY. Nathan's roster featured singers named Hawkshaw, Cowboy, Bull Moose, Lazy Jim, Ivory Joe, Bubber, Cleanhead, Texas Ruby, Lucky, Moon, and Grandpa, to name a few. But King Records' real strength remained in a man with no gimmick in his name—James Brown. He and the Famous Flames released single after single and helped King Records remain in business through the 1960s. "The company depended on him," Kessel said.

Due mainly to Brown's surging sales as well as Nathan's return to the office after a struggle with heart trouble, King Records was rated No. 5 among labels with the most nationally charted records in 1961, according to the Nashville trade magazine *Music Reporter.*

Sadly, Sydney Nathan died of heart disease in Miami on March 5, 1968. His business partners realized that he alone had the vision to guide the company. So they sold it. Soon King merged with Starday Records in Nashville to create Starday-King. The Cincinnati office, where James Brown operated a production company, was closed in 1971. His contract was sold to Polydor Records of New York.

In 1973, King Records was sold to the owner of Nashville's Gusto Records, which still owns the old label and reissues its classic recordings.

Since then, however, King's Cincinnati connections have slowly generated renewed interest. The sounds of James Brown's many sidemen—including Bobby Byrd on organ, a young William "Bootsy" Collins on bass, and Beau Dollar on drums—intrigue music lovers around the world. And King's list of eclectic acts continues to fascinate people who enjoy everything from jazz to rockabilly.

On November 24, 2008, the Rock 'n' Roll Hall of Fame and the city joined together to erect a marker at 1540 Brewster Avenue, commemorating Cincinnati's most important record company. A thankful crowd applauded that chilly day, but they also understood that the best lasting memorial already exists in the music itself.

King Records will always be the king of roots.

One

HILLBILLY BOOGIE

Lloyd "Cowboy" Copas, a native of Adams County, Ohio, sang on WLW's *Boone County Jamboree* and on WSM's *Grand Ole Opry* with Pee Wee King's Golden West Cowboys. King Records signed him in 1945. The next year, he hit nationally with "Filipino Baby." (Author's collection.)

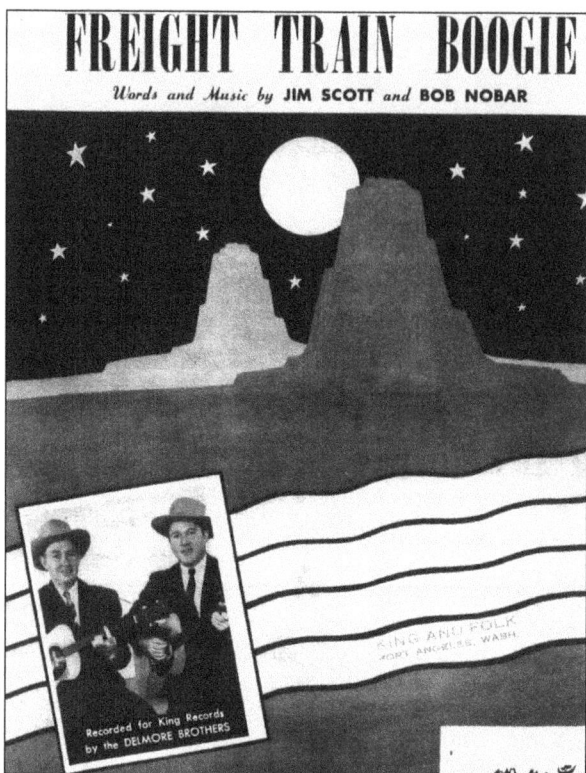

FREIGHT TRAIN BOOGIE

Words and Music by JIM SCOTT and BOB NOBAR

Recorded for King Records
by the DELMORE BROTHERS

Alton and Rabon Delmore, the influential Delmore Brothers, cut "Hillbilly Boogie" and "Freight Train Boogie" for King Records in 1946. Their expert songwriting and musicianship helped establish the label's fresh hillbilly sound. (Courtesy of Deborah Delmore.)

The Alabama natives were working as staff musicians at WLW when Syd Nathan signed them and gave their music a harder edge. By then, they were not newcomers to the music business. They had already played on the *Grand Ole Opry* and recorded for Bluebird and other labels. In 1949, they wrote and recorded—in King Records' own studio—their biggest hit, "Blues Stay Away From Me." (Author's collection.)

KING

THE 'KING' OF THEM ALL

MADE I U.S.A.

(1972)

Vocal with
Instrumental Trio

HILLBILLY BOOGIE
(Rabon Delmore)
DELMORE BROTHERS
527-A

Alton (left) and Rabon Delmore were versatile enough to sing, write, and entertain on WLW. They joined fellow station employees Grandpa Jones and Merle Travis to round out the Brown's Ferry Four, a gospel group that later recorded for King. The c. 1944 advertisement below, one of King Records' earliest, shows a small sketch of the factory in Evanston and announces new country records—then called hillbilly—for Grandpa Jones, the Carlisle Brothers, Bill and Evalina, Hank Penny, and others. Note the stereotypical long-bearded hillbilly character and the smiling jukebox. In the early years of King Records, Nathan actively sought help from the jukebox industry to bring his records before the public. His slogan was "If it's a King—it's a hillbilly." Soon he would campaign to change the name to country music. (Right, author's collection; below, courtesy of Zella Nathan.)

Sincerely
Alton & Rabon
Delmore

Exclusive **KING** Recording Artists **KING** RECORDS

NOW I CAN HEAR SOME GOOD OLE HILL-BILLY TUNES!!!

ANNOUNCEMENT
TO THE TRADE

WE ARE HAPPY TO ANNOUNCE THE NEW KING RECORDS, MANUFACTURED IN OUR OWN PLANT. A NEW LABEL—A NEW FACTORY—A NEW POLICY.

. . . OUR POLICY

IF IT'S A KING—IT'S A "HILL-BILLY" AND WE MEAN IT! NOTHING BUT HILL-BILLY RECORDS WILL BE MANUFACTURED BY US UNDER THE KING LABEL, AND OUR STAFF OF HILL-BILLY COMPOSERS ARE EXERTING EVERY EFFORT TO WRITE THE KIND OF TUNES YOUR CUSTOMERS WANT TO HEAR.

THOSE KING RECORDS WILL SURE BRING IN THE NICKELS

KING
It's Raining Here This Morning
I'll Be Around If You Need Me
Grandpa Jones
502

KING
Sweet, Sweet Thing
Prisoner's Farewell
Delmore Brothers
503

KING
Maggie, Get the Hammer
Why Should I Be the Only One To Care?
Carlisle Brothers
504

PRICE 75¢   COST 49½¢
Plus Tax   Not Including Tax
TERMS: C. O. D. F. O. B. CINCINNATI, O.

KING
Filipino Baby
I Don't Blame You Cowboy (Pappy)
Copas
505

SHIPPING DATE DECEMBER 1ST

KING
Won't You Take Me Back!
Good-Bye Booze
Bill and Evalina
506

KING
Tear Stains on Your Letter
Last Night
Hank Penny
507

KING RECORD CO.
1540 BREWSTER AVE. CINCINNATI 7, OHIO
KINDLY SHIP C. O. D. THE RECORDS CHECKED

Quantity		Quantity	
502		505	
503		506	
504		507	

NAME ....
ADDRESS ....
CITY ....
STATE ....

ORDERS FILLED AS RECEIVED

FOUR NEW RELEASES MONTHLY

HOME OF KING RECORDS

KING RECORD CO.
1540 BREWSTER AVE.   CINCINNATI 7, OHIO

KING RECORDS

Syd Nathan achieved a successful and complete career redo, the first of many for him, on the veteran Delmore Brothers. Alton (left) and Rabon started on Columbia Records in 1931, cutting four sides, and then joined the *Grand Ole Opry* in 1932. They performed on the air for seven years. They switched to RCA-Victor's Bluebird label for the next nine years, cutting 20 sides a year. In 1940, when they were well-known performers, they moved to Decca Records, recording 25 sides that year. By the time they were accompanying shows on WLW Radio in Cincinnati, their recording career had declined. But Nathan had faith in them. He signed them to a long-term contract with his new King Records in 1944. After they hit with King, they went to work for Memphis radio station WMC. (Author's collection.)

Country singer Bob Newman sang with the Georgia Crackers of Columbus, Ohio, before signing as a solo artist with King Records. In 1950, King Records released his "Cry Baby Blues" and "One and One Is Two, Baby." He later became known for truck-driving records. (Author's collection.)

One And One Is Two, Baby

By LEE ROBERTS   PRICE 40¢

Featured and Recorded by
BOB NEWMAN

TANNEN MUSIC, INC.   146 WEST 54TH STREET, NEW YORK 19, N.

Dee Jay KING Special

QUARANTINED LOVE
(Roberts-Mathias)
BOB NEWMAN

(NOT FOR RESALE)
(Tannen-BMI)   Time: 2:24

Bob Newman's first solo record, CRY BABY BLUES and ONE AND ONE IS TWO, MY BABY, clicked big, and he followed that with an even bigger recording of LONESOME TRUCK DRIVER'S BLUES and LEFTOVER HASH. Now he is in big demand.
Vocal by Bob Newman
With String Band
959-A
(3090)

The 78-rpm record pictured here, Newman's "Quarantined Love," shows another of Nathan's innovations, the bio disc. He printed brief biographies of artists on promotional records, and sent them to disc jockeys and decision makers in the music business. The idea must have worked, for King Records continued to issue bio discs into the 1960s. (Author's collection.)

13

In 1953, Alabama disc jockey Jack Cardwell recorded two hits for King Records. He made the first, "The Death of Hank Williams," in Mobile to exploit Williams's fame. King ordered its pressing plant into hyperdrive. Williams died on January 1 of that year, and by February 14, Cardwell's record had already peaked at No. 3 on *Billboard's* best-selling country chart. (Author's collection.)

At the time, Williams's popularity was running so high that the sheet music publisher decided to place his photograph, not Cardwell's, on the cover. (Ironically, a physician named P. H. Cardwell gave Williams a couple of shots of morphine before the singer died.) Jack Cardwell's second and last hit for King Records—or any other company—was "Dear Joan," a No. 7 hit that summer. He then fell from the charts and into the abyss of musical obscurity. (Author's collection.)

14

After Harold "Hawkshaw" Hawkins returned from the army in World War II, he sang in talent contests and appeared on WWVA's popular *Jamboree*. One day, he sent a cheaply made demo to Syd Nathan, who nearly threw it away. Fortunately for the world, Nathan decided to listen to the shabby disc. The King Records chief then arranged to meet Hawkins and record four songs in a West Virginia radio station. Nathan once recalled, "The station was so small that I had to put the bass player in a closet and close the door because [by] even playing soft in this room, which was seven by seven feet, it was impossible to hear anything but the bass." The much-shorter Nathan could not have missed the Hawk, who stood nearly six feet, five inches in his cowboy boots. He was known for his friendly personality, which led people to call him "Eleven Yards of Personality." Nathan must have rejoiced upon signing yet another fanciful nickname. Hawkshaw and Cowboy Copas remained the bedrock of King Records' country roster into the early 1950s. (Author's collection.)

Kentucky natives Merle Travis and Louis "Grandpa" Jones were the first artists to join King Records. Travis became the one that got away. He quit his job on WLW's *Boone County Jamboree* and left for California. The move proved fortuitous. He sang the *From Here to Eternity* theme, wrote "Sixteen Tons," and became a respected guitarist. In 1946, he recorded "Cincinnati Lou," on Capitol Records. (Author's collection.)

Dealers! ARE YOU GETTING ALL THE RECORDS YOU NEED OF THESE KING HILLBILLY HITS?

KING LEADS THE HILLBILLY PARADE!

★ **KING 505**
FILIPINO BABY
I DON'T BLAME YOU
Cowboy Copas

★ **KING 527**
HILLBILLY BOOGIE
I'M SORRY I CAUSED
YOU TO CRY
Delmore Bros.

★ **KING 535**
RAINBOW AT MIDNIGHT
DON'T TELL ME
YOUR WORRIES
Bill Carlisle

★ **KING 570**
FREIGHT TRAIN BOOGIE
SOMEBODY ELSE'S DARLING
Delmore Bros.

★ **KING 578**
NEW PRETTY BLONDE
(New Jole Blon)
WHEN A SOLDIER KNOCKS
AND FINDS NOBODY HOME
Moon Mullican

★ **KING 598**
KENTUCKY WALTZ
HEARTACHES
Cowboy Copas

Write, wire or phone
KING RECORD DISTRIBUTING CO.

This *c.* 1946 advertisement promoted King's hillbilly releases from a different address—1538 Brewster Avenue, Cincinnati 7, Ohio. The building in which King Records operated was actually several buildings, all connected. Apparently two of them used different street numbers. When the company finally took over most of the complex, it simplified the address to 1540. The "7" was a pre–zip code identification number. (Courtesy of Zella Nathan.)

Carolina Cotton, another early King Records country artist, hosted a program twice a week on the Armed Forces Radio Services in the late 1940s and early 1950s. She called herself the "Girl of the Golden West" and the "Queen of the Range." Her show *Carolina Cotton Calling* entertained 90 million overseas listeners. She received more fan mail than any Hollywood star to appear on the Armed Forces Radio Services. (Author's collection.)

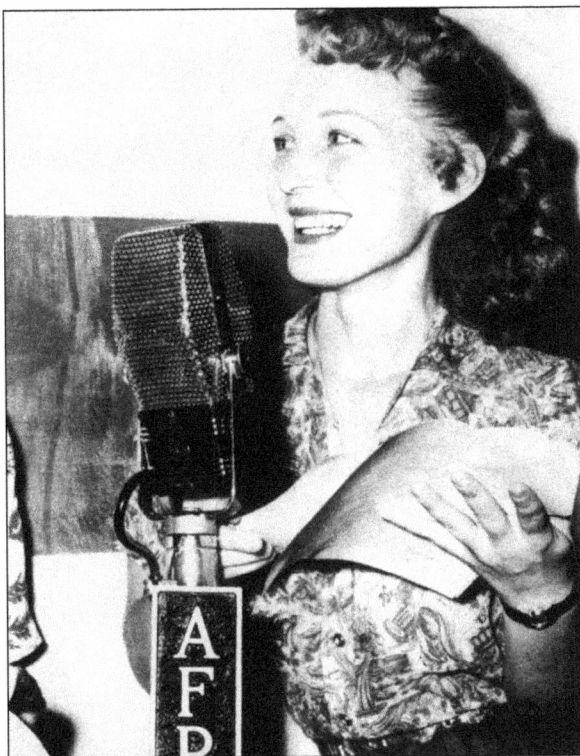

In 1938, an announcer forgot the names of Henry D. Hayes and Kenneth C. Burns, who appeared on Chicago's WLS *Barndance* and Don McNeil's *Breakfast Club*. So the announcer called them Homer and Jethro. The name stuck. They recorded for King Records in 1947 and played on sessions. Their comic country act belied the fact that they were terrific musicians. They recorded "Donkey Serenade" and other humorous songs. (Author's collection.)

17

Pianist Henry "Redd" Stewart of Tennessee started performing in Pee Wee King's Golden West Cowboys in 1940. They became songwriting partners, turning out hits such as "The Tennessee Waltz." Stewart recorded a number of songs for King Records in the late 1940s and early 1950s. (Author's collection.)

This picture shows that Stewart and his Kentucky Colonels recorded other people's material. This song, "If You'll Come Back To Me," is credited to Syd Nathan and Dewey Bergman, King Records' pop music director. Usually Nathan wrote under the pseudonym Lois Mann. He dabbled on the piano and thought of song ideas while walking through the halls of the King factory. "I write all the way down the line—from a pop tune to a hillbilly to a risqué, double entendre," he once said. "I cover the field pretty well." (Author's collection.)

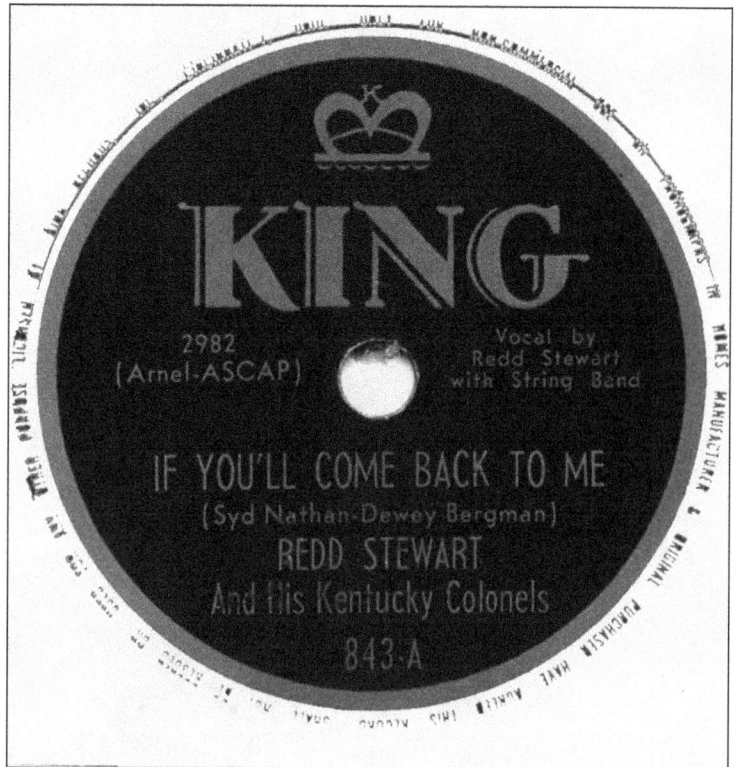

In November 1943, Grandpa Jones and fellow WLW sideman Merle Travis accompanied Nathan to Dayton, Ohio, to record Grandpa's original "The Steppin' Out Kind." For King Records' first release, Nathan billed the duo as the Shepherd Brothers. In this rarely seen photograph, Jones is performing out of character. People in Cincinnati probably did not recognize him when he walked near Crosley Square. (Author's collection.)

Seen here, the original old-timer himself—singer, songwriter, and banjo player—poses in character next to a King Records microphone. After Grandpa Jones returned from World War II, he rejoined King and left WLW. "I just wanted to pick on a label," he said. Nathan recorded him in Cincinnati, Hollywood, Chicago, and other cities. One of his more warmly received records was "It's Raining Here This Morning." (Author's collection.)

West Virginian Charlie Gore started on WLW-T's *Midwestern Hayride* in 1949 and became a regional country star. He recorded for King from 1951 to 1956, during which time he cowrote Bonnie Lou's hit "Daddy-O." Gore fit Syd Nathan's idea of well-rounded talent—a country performer who could write commercially, play well, sing, and entertain. (Courtesy of Steve Lake.)

Gore and his band perform on a television benefit show in Indiana around 1956. He used no drummer, only a guitar, upright bass, fiddle, and accordion. In 1953, Gore left the *Hayride* to start the similar *Indiana Hoedown* in Indianapolis. He left that show in 1959 and retired from music. (Courtesy of Steve Lake.)

20

Gore sings as his band performs in a small-town Indiana school gymnasium around 1955. After coming out of retirement in 1960, he became a disc jockey for WVOW in Logan, West Virginia, and was elected to the state legislature for one term. He later returned to the Cincinnati area. He could not stay away from the crowds. In 1963, he opened a Columbus nightclub called the Frontier Ranch with Ray Stingley and later rejoined the *Hayride* in Cincinnati. By then the show was being broadcast in color and syndicated by ABC Films to 56 markets. When his television days ended, he remained in greater Cincinnati and served on the Butler County Board of Elections. (Courtesy of Steve Lake.)

King Records owed its early successes to three major things—proper timing (the postwar market needed new country acts); talented performers, writers, and executives; and sufficient trade advertising. This advertisement from around 1946 promotes two performers whose music sounds good to this day—Hank Penny and Bill Carlisle. Penny cut many songs with novelty titles, and Carlisle followed his hit "Rainbow at Midnight" with his own 1947 answer record, "Answer to Rainbow at Midnight." (Courtesy of Zella Nathan.)

Bill Carlisle (at the microphone) was born in Wakefield, Kentucky, in 1908. He came from a musical family; brother Cliff became a country star and Bill led the Carlisles with sister Betty. As a child, Bill taught himself to play guitar. In 1931, he started in Louisville radio, and two years later he was recording in New York. He joined King Records in the mid-1940s. (Author's collection.)

Recording exclusively on
KING Records

After Hank Penny became a popular Cincinnati radio performer, he moved to California in 1945 and cultivated a new audience with his band, the California Cowhands. The Birmingham native often dressed in a cowboy suit decorated with shiny pennies for buttons. For King Records, he recorded songs such as "Bloodshot Eyes" and "Won't You Ride In My Little Red Wagon." (Author's collection.)

23

Curly Fox—born Arnim Le Roy in Dayton, Tennessee—and his wife, "Texas Ruby" Owens, performed on radio stations across the country, including WLW. They started recording for King Records in the late 1940s. Later the company issued albums by the duo with themes such as railroad songs, Nashville songs, and square dance songs without calls. (Author's collection.)

Wayne Raney became one of King Records' top session players, songwriters, and artists of the late 1940s. The native of Wolf Bayou, Arkansas, started playing harmonica as a child. He hitchhiked across the country until a radio station manager hired Raney to perform on a program. In Cincinnati, he hosted the *Jamboree* on WCKY. His biggest King hit was "Why Don't You Haul Off and Love Me," in 1949. (Author's collection.)

Two

BLUES ON BREWSTER

The "5" Royales featured cousins Lowman and Clarence Pauling and Johnny Tanner, plus Obediah Carter and Johnny Moore. In 1957, they hit with "Tears of Joy" and "Think." They often sang Lowman "Pete" Pauling's original songs, including "Dedicated to the One I Love," later a hit by the Shirelles. (Author's collection.)

Roy Brown, a popular songwriter and pianist from New Orleans, sang in clubs on the Gulf Coast. He wrote and recorded the seminal "Good Rockin' Tonight" for DeLuxe Records in 1948, shortly before King Records acquired the company. He and his band, the Mighty, Mighty Men, turned out hits consistently for the independent label through 1951. (Author's collection.)

ROY BROWN

DOES IT AGAIN!

LONG ABOUT SUNDOWN

and

CADILLAC BABY

DeLuxe 3308

MAKES THREE (3) IN A ROW

DeLuxe 3306	DeLuxe 3304
DREAMING BLUES	**HARD LUCK BLUES**
LOVE DON'T LOVE NOBODY	NEW REBECCA

KING RECORDS

This 1950 advertisement touts Brown's "Long About Sundown" and "Cadillac Baby." Brown usually recorded at engineer Cosimo Matassa's little studio in New Orleans. Later Brown would travel to Cincinnati to make music at King Records—the place where the blues met the big beat. (Author's collection.)

26

At New Orleans's Dew Drop Inn in 1948, Brown asked Wynonie Harris, a fellow blues shouter, to record "Good Rockin' Tonight," but Harris declined. Before Brown could cut the song, however, Harris recorded it in King Records' new studio in Cincinnati. The two versions battled for airplay on *Billboard*'s chart. First Harris peaked at No. 1. A couple of weeks later, Brown's version hit No. 13. (Author's collection.)

ONE NIGHT ONLY!
"GOOD ROCKIN"
WYNONIE HARRIS
"MR. BLUES"

PITTSBURGH COURIER POLL WINNER AS

Nation's Favorite

BLUES SINGER

Latest recordings: "Grandma Plays the Numbers", "I Feel that Old Age Coming On"

WYNONIE HARRIS

EXTRA ADDED ATTRACTION
DUD BASCOMB And His Band

CLUB RIVIERA
SUN. NIGHT, MAY 29

Wynonie "Mr. Blues" Harris sang with Lucky Millinder's big band before signing with King as a solo act. He recorded a number of R&B hits for the label from 1948 to 1952. He cut the less successful "Big Old Country Fool" in New York in 1957. It came from Syd Nathan's large Lois Music catalog. (Author's collection.)

In 1947, King Records signed Texas pianist-vocalist Ivory Joe Hunter, who had already cut two top-10 blues hits for other labels. Among the seven hits he recorded for King, the most recognizable is "Jealous Heart," recorded in 1949. (Author's collection.)

Hunter went on to record hits for Atlantic, "Since I Met You Baby" and "Empty Arms." He became among the most popular of the black stars. Sadly, in late 1958, the hits stopped coming. (Author's collection.)

YOU HAVE UNTIL, —
SATURDAY, APRIL 23
TO WITNESS THIS GREAT NEW SHOW
JORDAN W. CHAMBERS'
★ ★ CLUB ★ ★
RIVIERA
4460 DELMAR BLVD.   JE. 8888
PRESENTS
IVORY JOE HUNTER
Singing "Pretty Mama," "Don't Fall in Love with Me," 'Siesta for Sonny'
PLUS THESE GREAT STARS
RETURNED BY POPULAR DEMAND
RED SAUNDER'S ORCHESTRA
PLUS
COOK & BROWN   VIOLA KEMP
Delightful Comedians   Body Beautiful
AND STARRING THE SENSATIONAL
RIMMER SISTERS
Spider Burks 'M.C.'
2 BIG THRILL PACKED SHOWS NITELY 2

Mickey and Sylvia—McHouston Baker and Sylvia Vanderpool—are better known for their No. 1 RCA-Victor hit "Love Is Strange" in 1956. But they later signed with King Records, for which guitarist Mickey had played on sessions. Their King Records period—uneventful as it was—came in the late 1950s and early 1960s when they recorded as a duo and Mickey as a solo act. In 1962, Mickey recorded "No Name" for the Versailles label in Paris, and leased the single to King Records. Sylvia's big solo hit would come on her own independent label, Vibration Records, in 1973—the sexy "Pillow Talk." (Author's collection.)

Alfonso "Sonny" Thompson, a Chicagoan known early on for his Miracle Records hit "Long Gone," came to King Records when Syd Nathan bought the Miracle masters. Nathan appreciated Thompson's keyboard and arranging skills and used him for years as a recording artist and an A and R man in King's Cincinnati and New York offices. In Cincinnati, he played on Freddy King's "Hide Away" instrumental in 1960. These photographs show one of Thompson's extended play albums, and his No. 5 hit "I'll Drown In My Tears," written by King Records' A and R chief Henry Glover and sung by Thompson's wife, Lula Reed. Her vocal abilities were highly respected in the record industry. (Author's collection.)

Thompson and Reed recorded tracks in Cincinnati, New York, and Los Angeles with Thompson on piano. This poster, issued by their booking agent, shows them as a touring team too. Reed was an innovative singer from Port Clinton, Ohio, but not a hit act on her own. She gained notoriety for singing on her husband's 1952 King Records hit "Let's Call It a Day." (Author's collection.)

Jack: 8,000 of these are being mailed out by Gold's, too!

Come In and Visit Our New RECORD DEPT.

FREE! STORAGE ALBUM WITH PURCHASE OF $10!

Hear The Great

Well, Oh Well

By Tiny "Gravy Train" Bradshaw

Many other Blues, Jazz and Bop Records by
Memphis Slim, Joe Thomas, Wynonie Harris

5 RECORDS FOR $1.00

Reg. 89c and 79c Records

I LOVE YOU YES I DO
ALL MY LOVE BELONGS TO YOU
KING RECORDS
BULL MOOSE JACKSON
A FOOL IN LOVE

GOLD'S 1207 E. Washington Blvd.
at Central Ave.

Still goin' strong!

QUEEN RECORD 4116

"I KNOW WHO THREW the WHISKEY IN THE WELL".

by

Bullmoose Jackson

KING *Record Company*

1540 BREWSTER AVE.   CINCINNATI 7, OHIO

In late 1949, 8,000 copies of these postcards were sent to music people to promote Bull Moose Jackson's records as well as those by Tiny Bradshaw and other King acts. Benjamin "Bull Moose" Jackson, a Cleveland native who sang and played sax, joined Lucky Millinder's band in 1943 and thus came to King's attention. He started a backup band called the Buffalo Bearcats. His first hit was the answer song, "I Know Who Threw the Whiskey in the Well," which appeared on King Records' new Queen Records subsidiary label in the spring of 1946. At first, Queen Records was intended for black music only, but soon it was used for other kinds. Overshadowed by the more powerful King name, Queen Records was officially discontinued after about a year, although it was briefly revived in the 1960s. (Courtesy of Zella Nathan.)

32

Singer-pianist Amos Milburn from Texas was yet another Syd Nathan reclamation project. Nathan believed he could return older, once-established country and blues acts to the charts if his writers could compose catchy and modern songs for them. Milburn, best known for his No. 1 hit "Chicken Shack Blues" on Decca in 1948, certainly was bankable. Like many other once successful recording acts, including Lucky Millinder, Milburn joined King Records in hopes of reestablishing his recording career. Unfortunately what had worked a few years earlier for Millinder and Myron "Tiny" Bradshaw and others did not work for Milburn, Roy Milton, and other R&B music veterans who joined King Records in the late 1950s. Times had changed; the competition for airplay had become more intense. So the Milburn's Aladdin Records hits—made from 1948 to 1954—remain his last. (Author's collection.)

Tiny Bradshaw's band rocks the King Records recording studio in this c. 1950 photograph. Syd Nathan built the concrete-block studio in 1947, mistakenly on land that King Records did not own. Later he had to settle with the landlord. When tape debuted, the studio installed a one-track Ampex recorder, on which major blues and country hits were cut. (Courtesy of Howard Kessel.)

Youngstown native Tiny Bradshaw, a vocalist and pianist for black big bands, formed his first group in 1934. In 1950, he finally had a hit record at age 45, "Well Oh Well." It began a string of five for Bradshaw and King Records. When he died in 1958 at age 53, he was buried in Union-Baptist Cemetery in Cincinnati's Price Hill. (Author's collection.)

Alto saxophonist Tab Smith recorded the fine instrumental "Driving the Blues" in the label's Cincinnati studio in 1960. Although the North Carolina native deserved a better fate, the record did not return him to the charts. His earlier hits on Decca and United remain his only two chart appearances. (Author's collection.)

Earl Bostic, one of King's early instrumentalists, played flute, clarinet, and saxophone, but he is known better for his alto sax and clarinet recordings. His two King Records R&B hits, "Sleep" and "Flamingo," both in 1951, led to a long affiliation with King Records. He became a pop/jazz/R&B album artist, whose King LP sales continued into the 1960s. (Author's collection.)

Bostic's booking agency distributed this small poster to announce the Tulsa native's new record. Bostic was known as a technically fine musician, but some of his band members grumbled that he did not let them play enough on stage. He wanted to do most of the performing himself. (Author's collection.)

"I am very happy to announce that my new record release

earl BOSTIC

"VELVET SUNSET"
(Introducing The Three B's)

backed by

"LINGER AWHILE"

will be on the market May 16th."

earl BOSTIC
AND HIS ORCHESTRA
KING RECORDS

FOR AVAILABLE DATES, WIRE, WRITE, PHONE

UNIVERSAL ATTRACTIONS
347 Madison Avenue, New York 17, N. Y. • Telephone MUrray Hill 4-4122

Billy Ward and the Dominoes, one of King Records' biggest 1950s doo-wop acts, employed two R&B stars of the future for other record companies: Clyde McPhatter, who would sing with the Drifters and also become a solo act, and the great Jackie Wilson, who would record "Lonely Teardrops." This photograph shows Wilson on the far right. (Author's collection.)

A Terrific DOUBLE-HEADER!

TWO GREAT RELEASES
by KING

These releases are headed for top popularity — FAST! Two members of Lucky Millinder's orchestra in two terrific releases. Order yours NOW!

KING

BULL MOOSE JACKSON
KING 4181
I LOVE YOU YES I DO
BACKED BY
SNEAKY PETE

WRITE
WIRE
OR
PHONE ORDERS TODAY

PAUL BRECKENRIDGE
KING 4182
ROCK-A-MA SOUL
BACKED BY
LONESOME ROAD

KING RECORDS

OKLAHOMA CITY
LOS ANGELE
CHARLOTT
NEW YORI
CHICAG(
DALLA

EXECUTIVE OFFICES, 1540 BREWSTER AVE., CINCINNATI 7, OHIC

King RECORD DISTRIBUTING Co.

1540 BREWSTER AVE.   CINCINNATI 7, OHIO

Cleveland native Bull Moose Jackson had so many hits in King Records' early days (the first being on the Queen Records subsidiary) that the company decided to advertise him with other acts to help them sell more records. Unfortunately for Paul Breckenridge, the strategy failed. Jackson's first hit, "I Know Who Threw the Whiskey in the Well," answered Lucky Millinder's 1946 Decca song. Jackson came back with "I Love You, Yes I Do" in 1947. In a swinging big band style, Jackson sang and played sax on King Records hits through 1949, when his style started to sound stale. One hit was his risqué "I Want a Bowlegged Woman." He recorded it for the King Record Distributing Company. (Author's collection.)

Three

EVANSTON COUNTRY

In this *c.* 1948 photograph, Syd Nathan, center, holds court during a live WKRC radio broadcast presumably from a department store. Cowboy Copas is standing to the left of Nathan, Homer and Jethro to Nathan's rear, and Grandpa Jones to the right. Kneeling is disc jockey Nelson King, who provided much airplay during the early years. (Courtesy of Steven D. Halper.)

COPY CAT

Words and Music by FELICE and BOUDLEAUX BRYANT

AS RECORDED AND FEATURED BY COWBOY AND KATHY COPAS—KING RECORD No. 1034

60¢

SPIN MUSIC, INC.

Sole Selling Agents: KEYS MUSIC, INC.   146 West 54th Street, New York 19, N. Y.

Cowboy Copas and daughter Kathy recorded together for King Records. When she was a teenager in the early 1950s, they made "Copy Cat," written by the great Felice and Boudleaux Bryant. Kathy later married Randy Hughes, who would fly the airplane in which he, Cowboy, Hawkshaw Hawkins, and Patsy Cline died in a 1963 crash. (Author's collection.)

This c. 1945 photograph, taken at WLW, shows country singer Bonnie Lou at the microphone with the Trailblazers. Ray Sosby, a fiddle player, stands to the far left; Louis Innis, a guitarist and Bonnie's future A and R man at King Records, is second from right; and Leonard Sosby, a bass fiddle player, is on the far right. The man to the immediate left of Bonnie's is unidentified. (Courtesy of Toby Aydelott.)

Bonnie Lou came to Cincinnati from Kansas City to perform on WLW in 1945. She yodeled and sang on various programs. She left briefly, returned to the station, and became a mainstay of the *Midwestern Hayride* for two decades. In 1953, she recorded two national top 10 country hits for King Records: "Seven Lonely Days," a song also recorded by pop singer Georgia Gibbs, and "Tennessee Wig Walk." Bonnie is known also for her work on WLW-T, where she cohosted the *Paul Dixon Show* and appeared on Ruth Lyons's *50-50 Club*. (Author's collection.)

Clyde Moody, a native of North Carolina's Cherokee Reservation, started his career on the radio in Spartanburg and played with Joe Mainer's Sons of the Mountaineers and Bill Monroe before signing with King Records as a solo performer in the 1940s. He recorded the hits "Carolina Waltz," "Red Roses Tied in Blue," and "I Love You Because." Fans called him the "Hillbilly Waltz King." (Author's collection.)

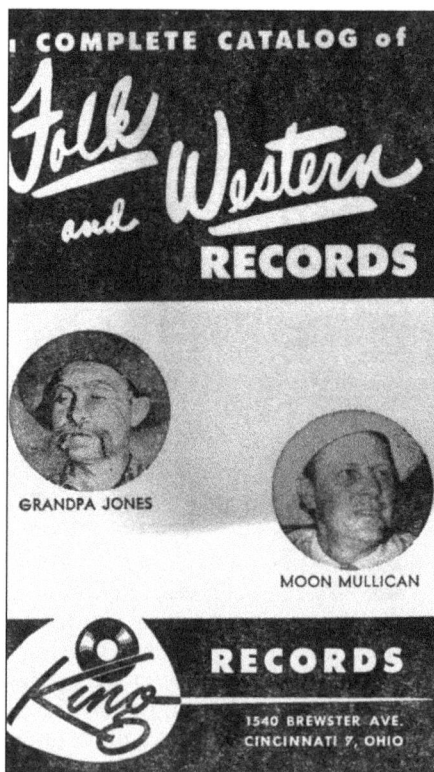

King Records issued this small catalog around 1947. In those days, folk and western were blurry terms. Western was known for western themes. Folk fell under the jurisdiction of hillbilly music, a name that Syd Nathan campaigned against. He claimed the term maligned the music. He preferred country music. This publication included 78-rpm discs by Moon Mullican, known as the "King of the Hillbilly Piano Players." (Author's collection.)

After leaving Mercury Records in 1955, the Stanley Brothers, Carter and Ralph, came to King Records—a coup because the popular bluegrass band was voted Best Instrumental Group that year. King continued to sell their records through the 1960s, and the band often recorded in the Brewster Avenue studio. In 1960, the brothers hit with "How Far to Little Rock." Ray Pennington produced some of their albums. (Author's collection.)

West Virginia's Bailes Brothers, Johnnie and Homer, wrote and recorded country and gospel songs for King Records from 1950 to 1954. In keeping with the times, one was called "Bull Frog Boogie" (King 1219). The group—two acoustic guitars, a fiddle player, and an upright bassist—continued to build a following through the Grand Ole Opry and KWKH in Shreveport. (Author's collection.)

His touring car looks a mile long, but then Doc Williams (second from right) and his band rode in style in the 1950s. He wrote songs for King Records' Lois Music, recorded for the record company, and performed on Wheeling's *Jamboree*. (Author's collection.)

In September 1947, radio stations played Fairley Holden's quintessential country title, "Keep Them Cold Icy Fingers off of Me." He recorded it in King's Cincinnati studio, and performed regularly on WIBW in Topeka, Kansas. Unfortunately too many disc jockeys kept their fingers off his record. (Author's collection.)

In the 1940s, King Records recorded its share of good fiddle players, whose songs were later issued on compilation albums and on singles. In this two-page layout in King's *Record Roundup*, the fiddlers play forever. Red Herron (far right) was well known for his flying fingers, and Margie Linville showed everyone just how good a woman could play. (Author's collection.)

Jimmie Osborne, known as the "Kentucky Folk Singer," hailed from Winchester. He played on the *Grand Ole Opry* and other barn dance shows. His King hits were "My Heart Echoes," 1947; "The Death of Little Kathy Fiscus," 1948; and "God Please Protect America," in 1950. He based "The Death of Little Kathy Fiscus" on a highly publicized fatal accident in which Fiscus was trapped in a well. (Author's collection.)

"Ramblin'" Tommy Scott came out of Athens, Georgia, to write and sing about people he met in the Great Smoky Mountains. He started performing on a small radio station in Athens, then left to appear on some of the largest stations in the nation. When he recorded for King Records in the early 1950s, he was also a star of the Wallace Brothers Circus. (Author's collection.)

Before joining King Records around 1947, Al Dexter—born Clarence Albert Poindexter in Roanoke, Virginia—recorded "Pistol Packin' Mama" and other hits. He wrote songs, played guitar and fiddle, and sang. Although he recorded no national hits for King Records, he added to the luster of the company's country music line. (Author's collection.)

Rome Johnson, of Winchester, Kentucky, performed every Saturday on WNOP in Newport, Kentucky. He learned to play guitar at age 15, and a few years later, he started writing songs and singing on WSMK in Dayton. The country singer regularly performed in Ohio and Kentucky in the late 1940s and early 1950s. His most popular King Records song was "Waltz of the Wind." (Author's collection.)

The York Brothers, Leslie and George, came from Louisa, Kentucky, in the Cumberland Mountains. They performed on radio stations in Denver and Portsmouth, Ohio, and on the *Grand Ole Opry*. After recording for the Universal label in 1939 and later Nashville's Bullet Records, they served in World War II. They signed with King Records in late 1947. (Author's collection.)

At a young age, Ann Jones sang on the radio with her sister in Kansas. She first recorded for King Records around 1952, when men dominated country music. She returned to King Records periodically to record through the early 1960s and developed a fan following out West. She once said she started writing songs because so many were written for men singers. She recorded "If I Was a Cat." (Author's collection.)

Wax is an old record industry term for early cylinder phonograph records. It will not go away. When shellac and vinyl record-manufacturing substances came into use over the years, writers continued to call discs "wax." (Perhaps because it rhymes with stacks.) This advertisement, published in 1948, announces the release of "Tennessee Moon" by Cowboy Copas and "Lollipop Mama" by blues shouter Wynonie Harris. (Author's collection.)

DYNAMITE ON WAX!
UP AND COMING KING HITS!

KING 718 PEACH TREE STREET BOOGIE
KING 4225 I WANT MY BABY
KING 4226 LOLLIPOP MAMA
KING 4230 I CAN'T GO ON WITHOUT YOU
KING 714 TENNESSEE MOON

ORDER NOW FROM YOUR NEAREST KING BRANCH.
KING 1540 BREWSTER AVE. CINCINNATI 7, OHIO

The Hometowners vocal group performed on WLW-T's *Midwestern Hayride* and sang backup on King Records sessions. Seen here are, from left to right, accordionist Buddy Ross, who appeared on various WLW-T shows; Jay Noaso; Freddie Langdon; and Kenny Price. Price was also a solo act who recorded hits for RCA-Victor in the 1970s, including "Too Big a Price to Pay" by Cincinnati musician Rollin Bennett Jr. (Courtesy of Donna Newman.)

This 45-rpm single, "Bully of the Town," was recorded in King Records' studio in 1963 and issued as a promotional bio disc, which gave interesting information to disc jockeys. Guitar wizard Joe Maphis wrote the song. He once performed on WLW's country music programs. (Author's collection.)

HILLBILLY IS KING EVERYWHERE!

Grandpa Jones, popular KING recording artist, has brought you hits like "Move It On Over" (665), "Mountain Dew" (624), "Don't Sweet Talk Me" (517), and "Old Rattler" (665).

Cowboy Copas's sensational KING records include "Signed, Sealed And Delivered" (658), "White Christmas" (675), "Honky Tonkin'" (657), and "Filipino Baby" (505).

The Delmore Brothers have made hits of these KING releases: "Boogie Woogie Baby" (599), "Freight Train Boogie" (570), "Harmonica Blues" (643), and "Barnyard Boogie" (664).

Homer and Jethro make a specialty of "corning up" the sweet songs. Have you heard their "Donkey Serenade" (659), "I Wonder Who's Kissing Her Now" (682), "Cielito Lindo" (615), and "Over The Rainbow" (596)?

Bill Carlisle's "Sparkling Blue Eyes" (656), "Rainbow At Midnight" (535), and "Answer To Rainbow At Midnight" (663), recorded for KING, are popular favorites of all.

Hank Penny's "Little Red Wagon" (639), "Flamin' Mamie" (534), and "Steel Guitar Polka" (639) for KING, have won many new friends for this popular artist.

Hawkshaw Hawkins has been recording exclusively for KING for a long time. "Mean Mama Blues" (563), "Try Me One More Time" (559), "Since You Went Away" (611), and "Sunny Side Of The Mountain" (667) are among his hits.

The Lightcrust Doughboys, top-notch Western recording and radio group, are now exclusively on KING releases. Hear their "Pappy's Banjo Boogie" and "It's A Dirty Shame" (681) today!

Moon Mullican's list of hits for KING are many, including "New Jole Blon" (578), "Jole Blon's Sister" (632), "Foggy River" (613), and "Sweeter Than The Flowers" (673).

The Shelton Brothers have reached new heights of popularity with KING records like "Deep Elm Boogie Woogie Blues" (660), and "Johnson's Old Grey Mule" and "It's No Use" (646).

Clyde Moody has been well-known on KING records for quite a while. Hear "Lonely Broken Heart" (637), "Shenandoah Waltz" (619), and "Next Sunday Is My Birthday" (671).

The York Brothers, newcomers to the KING label, are releasing popular hits in their inimitable style. Have you heard "Let's Don't Sleep Again" and "They Laid My Darling Away" (669).

KING RECORDS

OKLAHOMA CITY
NEW YORK CITY
LOS ANGELES
CHARLOTTE
CHICAGO
DALLAS

EXECUTIVE OFFICES, 1540 BREWSTER AVE., CINCINNATI 7, OHIO

Hillbilly is king at King, this c. 1949 advertisement proclaims, and it is correct. The company recorded and discovered a huge number of talented musicians and singers. If not for Nashville's music business politics, Sydney Nathan would be enshrined in the Country Music Hall of Fame. He is already in the Rock 'n' Roll Hall of Fame. (Author's collection.)

Texan Aubrey "Moon" Mullican, the "King of the Hillbilly Piano Players," started his solo career in 1946—just in time to sign with the relatively new King Records. He became known for his two-finger, right-hand style. He wrote and sang hits that included "New Pretty Blonde (Jole Blon)," "Sweeter than the Flowers," and "I'll Sail My Ship Alone." (Author's collection.)

JOLE BLON'S SISTER

by
MORRY BURNS
and
LOIS MANN

As Recorded by Moon Mullican
On KING RECORD 632

Lois MUSIC PUBLISHING CO.

Growing up near Laurel, Mississippi, in the 1930s, Luke McDaniel was so poor he could not afford an instrument. So he sold his only suit and spent his savings—seven dollars—to buy a mandolin. The King Records singer credited disc jockey Jack Cardwell with helping him get established in the business. (Author's collection.)

RENO & SMILEY AND THE TENNESSEE CUT-UPS

South Carolina bluegrass pioneer Don Reno, a former barber who played with Arthur Smith and the Crackerjacks, teamed with North Carolina entertainer Red Smiley to form Reno and Smiley and the Tennessee Cut-Ups in 1949. They signed with King Records in 1952, and continued to record for the label into the 1960s. Their presence (in addition to the Stanley Brothers) gave King two of bluegrass music's top acts. Reno played guitar, banjo, and harmonica. Their King Records hits were "Don't Let Your Sweet Love Die" and "Love Oh Love, Oh Please Come Home." This photograph shows the band around 1961 standing in front of their tour bus, ready to hit the highways. (Author's collection.)

52

Shorty Long came from Reading, Pennsylvania, and performed on the *National Barn Dance* in Chicago with the Santa Fe Rangers. He sang and played the fiddle and accordion. In the early 1950s, he played on sessions for King Records and recorded for the label. At 14 years old, he studied at the College of Rome, Italy, and graduated with honors as a violinist. (Author's collection.)

Cowboy Copas and Hawkshaw Hawkins turned over their fan club activities to Chaw Mank, who operated clubs for entertainers and wrote their fan newsletters. This one is from 1950. At his peak at that time, Copas was one of country music's hottest entertainers. (Author's collection.)

Harold "Hawkshaw" Hawkins was not far behind Cowboy Copas in fan appeal. Together they were two of country music's most talented and popular singers. Hawkshaw's hits started with "Pan American" in 1948 and abruptly ended at King with "Slow Poke" in 1951. He went eight years without a national hit until he found it with "Soldier's Joy." Interestingly, they both hit rough spots when country music suffered a brief decline in the early to mid-1950s. Both men jumped to Nashville labels, and both died in the plane crash that killed Patsy Cline in 1963. Three days before Hawkins would die, his comeback record, "Lonesome 7-7203," hit No. 1. The company? King Records. (Author's collection.)

Four

JAMES BROWN, R&B, AND JAZZ

James Brown smiles in this *c.* 1967 photograph, and he should. By then, he was carrying King Records on his muscular shoulders, and his major struggles with owners were history. "Soul Brother No. 1" would soon produce music for his own King Records–distributed labels. (Author's collection.)

JAMES BROWN

Recording Exclusively for
KING RECORDS

In the King Records' studio on February 6, 1956, James Brown and the Famous Flames recorded four songs, including his original "Please, Please, Please." It was mostly a moaning repetition of the three words—ghastly and foreign sounds to the ears of traditionalist Sydney Nathan, a genuine hook line admirer. "What in the hell are they doing?" he yelled in the control room. "That doesn't sound right to my ears." One can only imagine how Brown's guttural sounds grated on Nathan's weary soul that day. After spewing a few profanities, he reportedly told Brown and producer Ralph Bass, "Nobody wants to hear that noise." To Nathan's surprise, however, the record hit big. Suddenly Brown and the group had gained a reprieve at King's Federal Records subsidiary, operated by Bass. He knew his job was secure as long as the hits kept coming. (Author's collection.)

56

At times, Brown reached out to Nathan, and their often-contentious relationship went smoothly—for a time. Finally, after Brown proved that he could consistently sell millions of records, Nathan realized that it was futile to restrain such a popular act in the studio. From 1966 until 1968, the two patched their cracked relationship. (Author's collection.)

PRISONER OF LOVE

words and music by
LEO ROBIN, CLARENCE GASKILL and RUSS COLUMBO

Recorded by **JAMES BROWN**
and The Famous Flames
on KING Records

PRICE
75¢
U.S.A.
06212   09999

SHERWIN MUSIC INC.

After four modest sellers, in the spring of 1963 James Brown turned to an old pop ballad, "Prisoner of Love," which returned him to the R&B charts as well as the pop. The New York track balanced Brown's soulful moaning against Sammy Lowe's lush string arrangements. No doubt Nathan was pleased. Finally his style of song had been recorded by his top act. (Author's collection.)

Mr. Dynamite!
JAMES BROWN

latest album:
by James Brown
"PAPA'S GOT A BRAND NEW BAG"
KING 938

PAPA'S GOT
A BRAND
NEW BAG
KING 5999

Personal
Management:
Ben Bart
Records:
Bob Krasnow
Bookings:
Universal Attractic
200 W. 57th St.

In June 1965, Brown's pioneer funk single for King Records, "Papa's Got a Brand New Bag," reached the top 10 in R&B and pop. He and his band recorded it in an unlikely place—Arthur Smith's studio in Charlotte, North Carolina. Perhaps the site was chosen for convenience or to avoid anticipated criticism from King Records management. Smith, a veteran country musician, knew how to set up a studio. "It took only four tracks," Smith said of the "Papa" session, "because that's all we had. But the band was ready." The record's infectious dance beat and odd lyrics intrigued young listeners. Despite the limited number of tracks available, the recording's high level of clarity—and its musicianship—is still obvious. Many record buyers could not understand all the words on the hot new record, but they did appreciate Brown's electric performance. A year later, he and his band returned to Smith's studio to cut their hit "Don't Be a Drop-Out." (Author's collection.)

Erskine Hawkins recorded "Walkin' by the River," "The Way You Look Tonight," and other songs in New York in September 1952. The jazz artist would go on to carve out a career for himself in the field. He was one of a number of black jazz artists, including Roland Kirk, to record for King Records. (Author's collection.)

Like many other talented performers, singer-songwriter Joe Tex came to King Records before his time. In New York in 1955, he recorded "Come in this House" for the company, but he did not have the first of his many hits until 10 years later on the Nashville-based Dial label. He is known for "Hold What You Got" and "Skinny Legs and All." (Author's collection.)

During a slow period in the early 1960s, King Records started distributing Beltone and other independent record labels, which was odd, because King Records was never known for its lightning-quick distribution. Nevertheless, the new labels generated interest and helped bring much-needed hits to King Records. Indianapolis native Bobby Lewis, who had recorded for the Parrot label as early as 1952, cut two big R&B and pop hits, "Tossin' and Turnin'" and "One Track Mind" for Beltone in 1961. (Author's collection.)

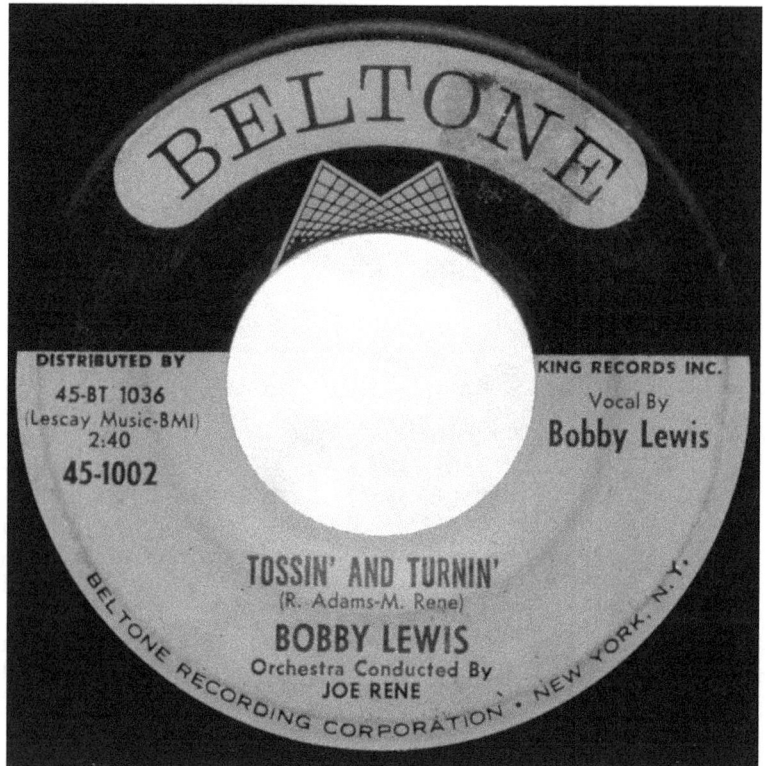

Lewis's hits brought King Records to the attention of rock disc jockeys across the nation. (Author's collection.)

The Platters, a smooth doo-wop group, started recording for Federal Records in 1954. The group cut "Only You," written by manager Buck Ram, but the record was not released, at least not in time to suit Ram. He moved his group to Mercury in 1955, reorganized its personnel and rerecorded "Only You" with lead Tony Williams. It became the first of 14 Platters hits through early 1960. (Author's collection.)

Lavern Baker, born Delores Williams in Chicago in 1929, performed with the Todd Rhodes Orchestra in 1952 and sang lead on "Trying" and three other King Records singles. By 1955, she had signed with Atlantic. She hit with "Tweedle Dee" and other songs through 1966, becoming yet another major R&B star who got away from King Records. (Author's collection.)

In 1950, Billy Ward formed the Dominoes in New York. Originally called the Ques, they were (in no particular order): Clyde McPhatter, lead vocals; Charles White, tenor; Bill Brown, bass; Joe Lamont, baritone; and Ward, piano. Ward signed with King Records that year, and the hits—10 altogether—began. Their second was one of King Records' double entendre songs called "Sixty-Minute Man," a highly suggestive song that would be covered and remade by many artists. McPhatter sang with Ward from 1950 to 1953. Jackie Wilson joined in 1953 and left in 1957. (Author's collection.)

In 1956, organist Bill Doggett liked a melody his band had created during a jam session. Soon a whole instrumental emerged, and the group recorded it in New York. "Honky Tonk (Parts I and II)" prominently featured Clifford Scott on sax, unlike most other Doggett recordings. The single became a huge R&B and pop hit that year. To maximize profits on the song, King asked Doggett to record a vocal version under his name with singer Tommy Brown. The hit helped make Doggett a major player in King Records' stable of instrumentalists. He was well represented on singles and albums, and "Honky Tonk" went on to influence a younger generation of musicians, including Cincinnati guitarist Lonnie Mack, who would record his guitar version for Fraternity Records. (Author's collection.)

A King Records talent scout discovered Otis Williams at a performance at Withrow High School. Williams and fellow students formed the Charms, an early doo-wop group. Their first hit, "Hearts of Stone," reached No. 1 on *Billboard*'s R&B chart in the fall of 1954 for King's DeLuxe Records. But Williams almost did not go into music. He was offered a football scholarship at the Ohio State University and a contract with the Cincinnati Reds. Music called, however, and soon the hits followed. After reorganizing in 1956, the group became Otis Williams and the Charms, and they hit with "That's Your Mistake," "Ivory Tower," and "United." Today Williams continues to perform and live in Cincinnati. In the *c.* 1956 photograph at left, group members are, from left to right, Lonnie Carter, Matthew Williams, Rollie Willis, Winfred Gerald, and Otis Williams in the middle. (Courtesy of Otis Williams.)

In 1961, Mississippi blues singer Albert King started a string of R&B hits with "Don't Throw Your Love on Me So Strong." It was his biggest record; King acquired it from the Bobbin label. Previously he had been with the Harmony Kings gospel group and Parrot Records. Later he signed with Stax Records. Here he poses with his Flying V. (Author's collection.)

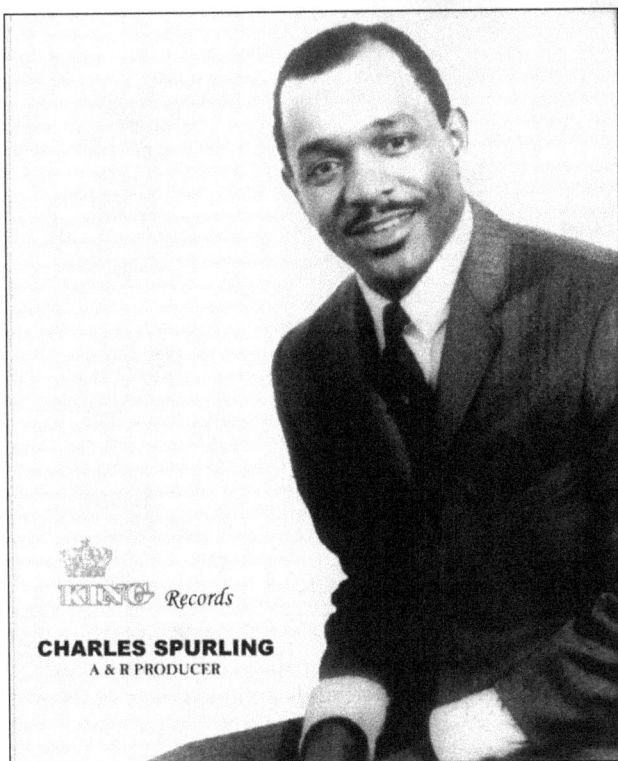

KING *Records*

CHARLES SPURLING
A & R PRODUCER

Charles Spurling of Lincoln Heights entered King Records as an A and R man in the mid-1960s. Soon he was recording his own singles and working with the Sisters of Righteous, a female vocal group from Cincinnati that sang on sessions and at times backed James Brown. One of Spurling's singles was "Popcorn Charlie." (Courtesy of Charles Spurling.)

Be sure to include these
James Brown Albums in
YOUR RECORD LIBRARY

1030 JAMES BROWN

1024 JAMES BROWN

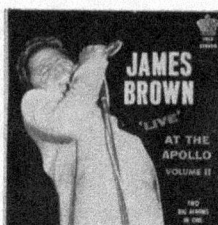
1022 JAMES BROWN

1020 JAMES BROWN

1018 JAMES BROWN

1016 JAMES BROWN

985 JAMES BROWN

961 JAMES BROWN

946 JAMES BROWN

938 JAMES BROWN

919 JAMES BROWN

909 JAMES BROWN

883 JAMES BROWN

851 JAMES BROWN

826 JAMES BROWN

804 JAMES BROWN

KING RECORDS, INC. ● 1540 BREWSTER AVE., CINCINNATI 7, OHIO

James Brown could not complain about a lack of publicity. King Records hawked and advertised him at every opportunity. This collage of colorful album covers—garish even in black and white reproduction—was printed on the back of a song folio. King Records designed most of its own album covers. Some of Brown's covers featured women wearing mini-skirts, go-go boots, and, yes, hot pants. (Author's collection.)

Brown's war for independence was not won with one hit record. He had to prove himself with every unusual track that he recorded. Naturally he clashed with Syd Nathan. It was not that Nathan had "tin ears," as some people assume. After all, the man founded the financially successful Lois Music, discovered talented songwriters, and personally oversaw hundreds of early country and blues sessions that yielded dozens of hits. After remastering many of King's early recordings in Nashville, engineer Mike Stone said, "On the tapes I could hear Mr. Nathan right there, behind the board, giving orders. He produced those early records." But Nathan's standard operating method—a song needs a catchy melody, a bridge, and an identifiable lyric line—was not necessarily Brown's. He dealt in riffs and beats. The two worlds clashed. (Author's collection.)

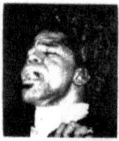

HOT! HOT! HOT!
ON KING RECORDS

JAMES BROWN

New Smash Single

"I Guess I'll Have to Cry, Cry, Cry"

King 6141

HANK BALLARD

Hot New Release

"I'm Back to Stay"

b/w

"Come on Wit' It"

King 6177

A JAMES BROWN PRODUCTION

The Sound of Success

KING RECORDS INC.

The summer of 1968 was "Hot! Hot! Hot!" In this advertisement, James Brown returns with "I Guess I'll Have to Cry, Cry, Cry"—his last period single with the Famous Flames. The record peaked at No. 15 on *Billboard*'s R&B charts. Ballard's record was not so fortunate. But he did return to the charts with "How You Gonna Get Respect (When You Haven't Cut Your Process Yet)," a single obviously aimed at R&B radio. It also peaked at No. 15, ironically, with the music of soulful white session players, the Dapps. Brown discovered the group in Cincinnati's Inner Circle nightclub and used the band on his and other performers' recordings. At various times the band included guitarist Troy Seals, who became a major Nashville songwriter; Tim Hedding, organ; Eddie Setser, guitar; Tim Drummond, bass; Les Asch, saxophone; and Beau Dollar, drums. (Author's collection.)

Hank Ballard's 1961 hit "The Switch-A-Roo" peaked at No. 26 on *Billboard*'s pop music chart. Its flip side, "The Float," also received enough airplay to break into the chart. (Author's collection.)

Although in later years Hank Ballard complained about Syd Nathan's management style, they both agreed to pose for this publicity shot in the early 1960s. By then, "The Twist" had brought Ballard much attention. Like Brown, Ballard was a top King Records act that remained under contract with the company for most of his long recording career, starting in 1953 and continuing until the label was finally sold again in 1971. And like Brown, his contract then went to Polydor Records. (Courtesy of Steven D. Halper.)

The Midnighters kick up their heels during a performance. They recorded a master tape of "The Twist" in King's Cincinnati studio on November 11, 1958. Chubby Checker's version, recorded in 1960 in Cameo Records' small studio in Philadelphia, essentially copied the King arrangement, with a slightly lighter feel. Checker also tinkered with the dance itself, making it look like he was putting out cigarettes with his feet. (Author's collection.)

In this c. 1960 photograph, Hank Ballard poses in front of a vocal microphone. In the late 1960s, he hired 16-year-old Bootsy Collins of Cincinnati and his band to back him on the road. Although Collins felt honored to perform on stage with the star, he also felt embarrassed when Ballard sometimes disappeared after shows—without paying the band. (Author's collection.)

Lucius "Lucky" Milllinder's biggest contribution to King was his band. In the 1940s, the Chicago-based entertainer permitted defections from trumpeter Henry Glover, who became a King Records A and R executive and songwriter—the most important behind-the-scenes leader, other than Nathan. Millinder himself had a big King hit in 1951—"I'm Waiting Just for You," with vocals by Annisteen Allen and John Carol. (Author's collection.)

Let's Hide Away
and
Dance Away
with

FREDDY
KING

(strictly instrumental

HIDE AWAY
SEN-SA-SHUN
SAN-HO-ZAY
SIDE TRACKED
WASH OUT
IN THE OPEN
HEADS UP
JUST PICKIN'
SWOOSHY
THE STUMBLE
OUT FRONT
BUTTERSCOTCH

Blues vocalist Freddy King, born Freddy Christian in Gilmer, Texas, holds his guitar. He recorded for Chess and other labels without much luck and sang in clubs and played on sessions in Chicago. In 1961, he came to King Records' studio to cut "Hide Away," a title inspired by a Chicago lounge. He followed with "Lonesome Whistle Blues," "San-Ho-Zay," and other Federal Records hits—six of them in only one year. Cincinnati musicians such as guitarist Lonnie Mack and organist Bob Armstrong acknowledge Freddy King's influence on local players during his short time in the city. The company also released an EP called *Hide Away*, which is highly collectible. (Author's collection.)

King Records' contributions to doo-wop are overshadowed by its country and blues efforts. The Swallows, the Platters, the Five Keys—actually, there were enough groups to start a whole company. In 1951, the Swallows hit with "Will You Be Mine." The Five Keys, from Newport News, Virginia, turned out hits with Capitol Records before joining King. Still, the group's less known King recordings are popular among collectors. (Author's collection.)

James Brown rocks onstage around 1968. When he was eight years old, he danced for National Guard soldiers, who threw him spare change. Later his fellow students paid to watch him dance. (Author's collection.)

By the late 1960s, James Brown was operating his own labels, including People Records, out of the King Records plant in Evanston, and recording his own artists as an independent producer. One of them was Vickie Anderson, with whom he did some recording. King Records A and R man Charles Spurling remembers her as being exceptionally talented. (Courtesy of Charles Spurling.)

James Brown Productions became an independent group within the King Records organization. This is one reason why Brown signed a new contract in 1966. Where else could he have received such a sweet deal? Brown ran his operation his way. He had his own A and R, promotional, and production people. He even put his picture on other acts' records. (Author's collection.)

In this *c.* 1967 photograph, Brown looks bewildered as he stands with a crown on head. The other people in the crowd are unidentified. The crown is fitting, however, for by that time his sales power was the force driving King Records. (Courtesy of Steven D. Halper.)

Detroit vocalist William Edgar "Little Willie" John—not to be confused with Federal Records' Little Willie Littlefield—became a solo R&B star for King Records in 1955 when he hit with "All Around the World." Other big hits included "Fever" and "Talk to Me, Talk to Me." While serving a prison sentence for manslaughter in 1966, he died of a heart attack. (Author's collection.)

NEW! KING SIZE SALES

HIDE AWAY
FREDDY KING
Federal 12401

LEAVE MY
KITTEN ALONE
LITTLE WILLIE JOHN
King 5452

HONKY TONK
BILL DOGGETT
King 5444

TONK GAME
HANK MARR
Federal 12400

WHEN I FALL
IN LOVE
ETTA JONES
King 5424

DEDICATED TO THE
ONE I LOVE
THE 5 ROYALES
King 5453

NEW! NEW! NEW!
LP'S WITH BUILT IN SALES

SPOTLIGHT ON
HANK BALLARD
HANK BALLARD AND
THE MIDNIGHTERS
King LP 740
(Let's Go Let's Go—Hoochie
Coochie Coo—etc.)

SURE THINGS
LITTLE WILLIE JOHN
King LP 739
(Sleep—Walk Slow—Heartbreak—
Cottage For Sale etc.)

BIG BEN'S BANJO'S
SING ALONG
King LP 2031
(30 d.j.'s favorite standard)

KING

This advertisement announces King Records' new singles and albums in early 1961. Organist Bill Doggett's often-recorded "Honky Tonk" is back, along with "Tonk Game" by his would-be successor, Hank Marr. Of course, fan favorite Little Willie John returns. (Author's collection.)

Talented Cincinnati jazz drummer Dee Felice—born Emidio DeFelice—played on sessions at King Records and recorded for the label's subsidiaries, often under the guidance of James Brown. One Felice album was called *In Heat*. In this c. 1968 photograph, Felice sports peace symbol cuff links—a symbol of the era. (Courtesy of Shelly Nelson.)

76

Five

KING'S LOST POP

In 1952, vocalist Mary Small recorded "You'd Think I Was in Love" in New York with her bandleader husband, Vic Mizzy. When she toured, he complained about what he called insufficient distribution. Mizzy, who shared credit on her King Records releases, later composed the theme for *Green Acres*. (Author's collection.)

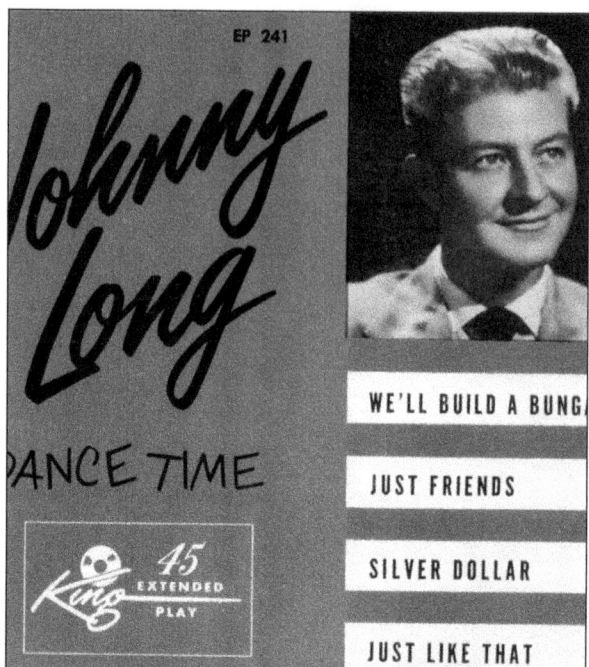

Unlike most pop artists who recorded for King Records, veteran bandleader Johnny Long often recorded in the Cincinnati studio, where he made "We'll Build a Bungalow." His most well received song was "Silver Dollar." Unfortunately by the time Long—and other pop performers—arrived at King Records, his recording career had cooled and big bands were losing out to the combo sound. But King performers had an even bigger problem. Their company was known for breaking blues and country records, not pop. King Records could not overcome this image issue. It was one thing to break a country record on a modest number of country radio stations but quite another feat to go after hundreds of pop music stations and compete head-to-head with the majors. (Author's collection.)

In 1952, high school singer Steve Lawrence recorded "Poinciana" for King Records in his native New York. Although King Records' shaky pop series was winding down, the company could not resist gambling on one more talented pop vocalist. The song did not suit Lawrence's youthful style, however, and King Records' A and R department could not match the quality of pop songs that Lawrence would record after leaving the label to join girlfriend Eydie Gorme on Coral Records in late 1956. His second Coral release—one of the biggest hits of his career—reached the top five; it was a pop cover of Buddy Knox's rockabilly hit, "Party Doll." From then on, Lawrence would start fulfilling the high expectations that King Records executives had for him with hits such as "Pretty Blues Eyes," "Footsteps," "Portrait of My Love," and "Go Away Little Girl." He would also appear on television and in films with Gorme, now his wife. (Author's collection.)

STEVE LAWRENCE'S LATEST SONG SUCCESS 1407

NEW POPULAR EDITION

POINCIANA

SONG OF THE TREE

Lyric by BUDDY BERNIER   Music by NAT SIMON

Recorded by
STEVE LAWRENCE
with
DEWEY BERGMAN'S
Orchestra on King Record 15185

Bob Kames was one of several pop organists who recorded albums for King Records in the 1950s and 1960s. Although Kames was not a part of King Records' official pop music offensive launched in 1949, he was definitely an adult pop act. He is remembered today as the man who made the chicken dance popular. (Author's collection.)

Elaine Gay recorded Henry Glover's "Rock Love" in 1954, but, as with many other King pop records, it failed to gain interest. The Fontane Sisters covered the song and took it to No. 13 in early 1955. They had done the same with "Hearts of Stone," the Charms hit, in 1954. They also would record cover hits of King's "Seventeen," "Daddy-O," and "Nuttin' for Christmas." (Author's collection.)

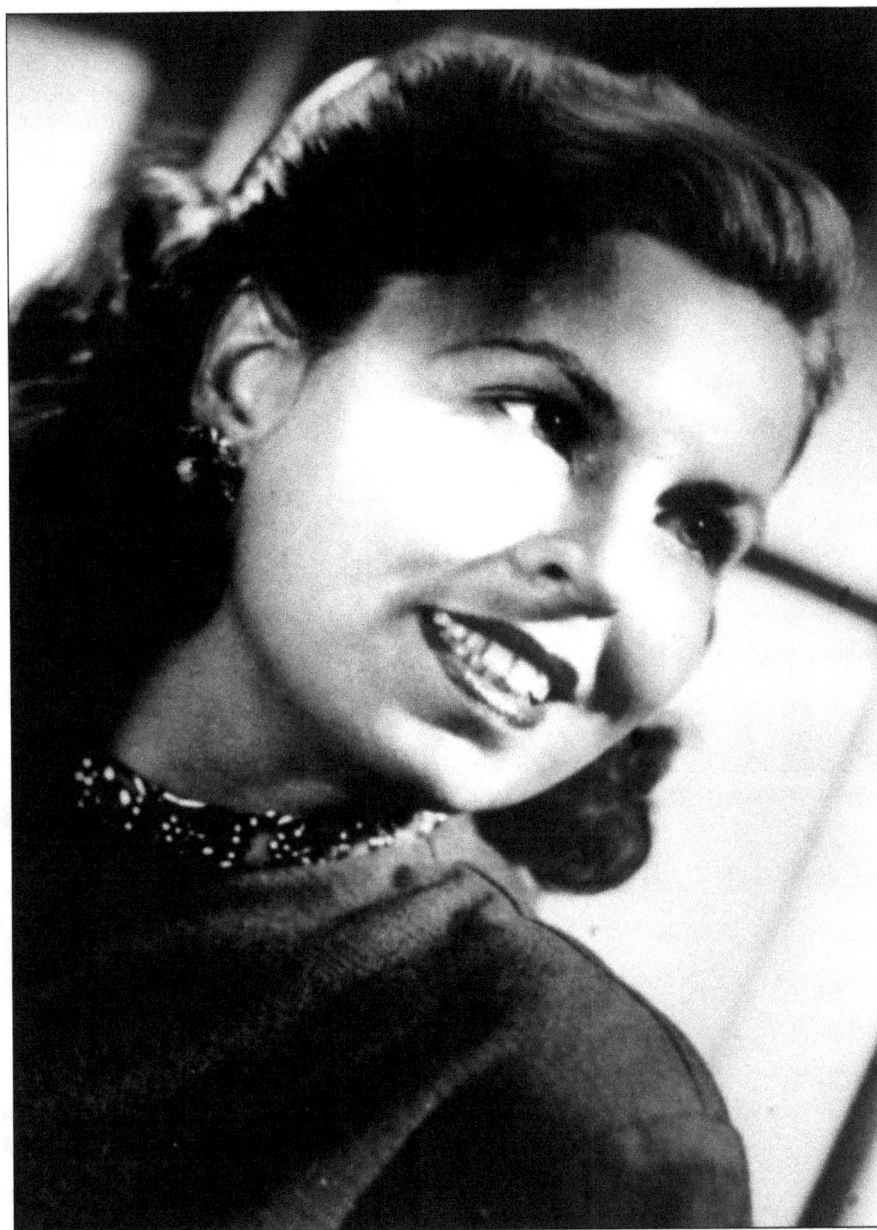

Pop vocalist Ruby Wright joined WLW and WLW-T in 1952 and hosted *Dixieland Unlimited*. The Anderson, Indiana, native remained on Cincinnati television for 20 years, much of it as a vocalist for Ruth Lyons's *50-50 Club*. Although Wright recorded only regional sellers for King through the 1950s, she did leave an impressive number of releases, including her most popular single, "Let's Light the Christmas Tree." Lyons wrote the moody holiday song, and Wright recorded it at the King Recording Studio. Then Syd Nathan "lent" Wright to his friend Harry Carlson at Cincinnati's Fraternity label. The record reached No. 41 on *Billboard*'s pop charts and became a huge hit in Ohio, Indiana, and Kentucky—where at noon the *50-50 Club* reigned as queen of weekday television. Wright returned to King Records and barely charted once, in 1959. Oddly enough, Carlson managed to achieve on a much lower budget what Nathan had failed to do—find success in pop music. (Author's collection.)

Excitement reigned at King Records in 1949, when it signed its first pop singer, young big-band vocalist Al Grant (born Al Cernik in Detroit). But Grant was not destined to be a star on King Records. After five consecutive singles failed, he left for Columbia Records. Producer Mitch Miller changed Grant's name to Guy Mitchell and recorded several hits with him, including "Singing the Blues," a No. 1 record. (Author's collection.)

This advertisement promoted Grant's singles "Cabaret" and "This Day Is Mine." Dewey Bergman, A and R chief for the new pop division, oversaw production. Grant's failure started King Records' pop experiment on a sour note, from which it never recovered. (Author's collection.)

Ulysses S. Grant . . . took only Richmond

AL GRANT
TAKES AMERICA
WITH FOUR GREAT RECORDINGS
CABARET
I DO, I DO, I DO
KING   15004
THIS DAY IS MINE
LOVER'S GOLD
KING   15005
AL GRANT with Dewey Bergman's Orchestra

NEW MINUTE MAN

Elliot Lawrence

and his orchestra
now record exclusively for *King*

the current
great blues
hit! . . . .

originally written
and recorded on
Federal Records by
THE DOMINOES

"SIXTY MINUTE MAN"

backed by 'QUICK'

Get this release
QUICK
QUICK
QUICK

King 15115

DISTRIBUTED BY

 **RECORDS, INC.**

General Offices:
1540 BREWSTER AVE.
CINCINNATI 7,
OHIO

Perhaps at Syd Nathan's urging, bandleader Elliott Lawrence recorded an unlikely pop version of the Dominoes' hit "Sixty-Minute Man." For once, Nathan must have reasoned, he would not be covered by another label. King Records would cover itself first. Of course, cover versions came anyway—by the Jive Bombers, Roberta Lee, and by other King acts. Lawrence's record remains a forgettable effort. (Courtesy of Zella Nathan.)

Clarinet player Larry Fotine, a Greek American named Fotinakis, arranged for Sammy Kaye's band and wrote hit songs. He formed his own band in 1948 and continued until 1954. He became another futile King Records pop act in 1950, employing the vocalist Cathy Cordovan. To Syd Nathan's frustration, ultimately she achieved more chart success than Fotine. As Cathy Carr, she returned to Cincinnati in 1956 with the big pop hit "Ivory Tower" on Fraternity Records. Nathan must have wondered how many promotion men Harry Carlson had working for him. The truth is, the friendly Carlson worked mostly alone on the telephone, talking with radio program directors across the country. (Author's collection.)

Bob Braun, of Ludlow, Kentucky, was not among King Records' initial wave of pop singers, but he recorded two such singles for the label, including "All My Love" in 1954. Since 1953, he had been appearing on WCPO-TV's popular *Pantomime Hit Parade* with Dotty Mack and Colin Male. Apparently this led King Records executives to believe the handsome Braun might be a good pop candidate. It must have frustrated Braun to pantomime other singers' hit records, but the show did start his long career in television. "All My Love" was not a national hit, but then King Records probably never expected it to be anything more than a regional one. Braun recorded only one more single for King Records, in 1959, before moving on to other labels. Then in 1962, he finally recorded a national hit—for Decca Records—called "Till Death Do Us Part." After appearing on Ruth Lyons's *50-50 Club* television show for years, until she retired in 1967, he succeeded her with the *Bob Braun Show* on WLW-T. (Author's collection.)

Originally Introduced by KAY ARMEN

COME ON-A MY HOUSE

Words and Music by ROSS BAGDASARIAN • WILLIAM SAROYAN

40¢
U.S.A.

Duchess

Kay Armen

As the line on top of her sheet music explains, Kay Armen introduced the hit "Come On-A My House." But that's all. Then the cover brigade descended to take away the song. Rosemary Clooney, a former Cincinnati singer now starring with Bing Crosby in the movies, had the biggest hit with the song. King Records' pop dream was thwarted again. (Author's collection.)

April Stevens—born Carol LoTempio in Niagara Falls, New York—was another King Records pop singer who eventually rediscovered the charts. When she joined the label around 1952, she had already recorded a hit for RCA-Victor. She recorded several King Records singles, including "Hot Tamale." When nothing happened, she left. In 1962 and 1963, she and brother Nino Tempo would record the hits "Deep Purple" and "Whispering" for Atco Records. (Author's collection.)

Ruth Lyons, a Cincinnati radio and television icon as well as a hit songwriter, was a favorite of Syd Nathan and other King Records owners. Although she did not record for the label, she had a history with it. (Author's collection.)

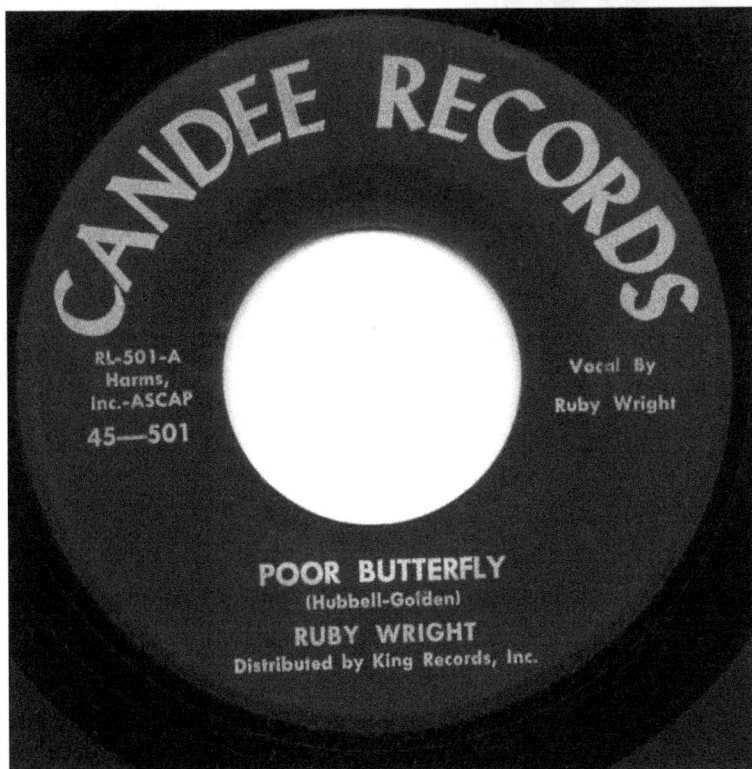

King Records briefly distributed Lyons's Candee Records, named for her young daughter, and pressed her records. She also recorded several Christmas albums in the King studio. (Author's collection.)

BLAZING THE TRAIL IN ALL THREE FIELDS

HANK PENNY

BULL MOOSE JACKSON

POPS

JOHNNY LONG
KING 15018 We'll Build a Bungalow
Skirts
KING 15035 Silver Dollar
Dixie
KING 15030 All the Way Choo Choo
University of North Carolina Medley
KING 15012 All the Bees Are Buzzin' 'Round My Honey
Signed, Sealed and Delivered

SISTER SLOCUM and "WOODY" BLOCK
KING 15023 I've Got Rings on My Fingers
Bye Bye Blues
KING 15020 Black and White Rag
I Ain't Got Nobody
KING 15026 Ja Da
Avalon

AL GRANT
KING 15019 Goodbye, My Love
Lovebirds

CARROLL LUCAS
KING 15021 The Wise Old Owl
If You Were Mine

FREDDIE MILLER and HIS DANCE MUSIC
KING 15031 Row, Row, Row
I Can't Make You

HILLBILLY

HANK PENNY I Was Satisfied
KING 828 Bloodshot Eyes
DELMORE BROTHERS Ain't Nothin'
KING 826 Troubles But the Blues
Pan American Boogie
KING 803 Blues, Stay Away From Me
Goin' Back to the Blue
Ridge Mountains

CLYDE MOODY I Love You Because
KING 837 Afraid
COWBOY COPAS The Gypsy Told Me
KING 825 Crazy Over You
MOON MULLICAN I'll Sail My Ship Alone
KING 830 Moon's Tune
RED PERKINS I Hate You
KING 836 Crocodile Tears
HAWKSHAW HAWKINS I Wasted a Nickel
KING 821 I'm Kissing Your Picture
Counting Tears
GRANDPA JONES I Do
KING 834 Daisy Dean
ZEB TURNER Why Don't You Haul Off
KING 845 and Get Religion
All Dressed Up

SEPIA

BULL MOOSE JACKSON
KING 4335 Must You Go?
Not Until You Came My Way
KING 4322 Is That All I Mean to You?
Why Don't You Haul Off
and Love Me?
LONNIE JOHNSON
KING 4336 Confused
Blues, Stay Away From Me
IVORY JOE HUNTER
KING 4326 I Quit My Pretty Mama
It's You, Just You
KING 4306 Guess Who
Landlord Blues
KING 4314 Jealous Blues
All States Boogie
WYNONIE HARRIS
KING 4330 Sittin' on It All the Time
Baby, Shame on You
EDDIE "CLEANHEAD" VINSON
KING 4331 I'm Gonna Wind Your Clock
I'm Weak But Willing
TINY BRADSHAW
KING 4337 Teardrops
Gravy Train
JOE THOMAS
KING 4299 Page Boy Shuffle
Teardrops

KING RECORDS

By 1950, King Records was promoting itself as the independent home of country, R&B, and pop music. But in truth, the company's only strength was in country and R&B. The pop music experiment would continue another year or so before quietly being discontinued. King Records never did learn how to promote pop records. But Syd Nathan and his executives never lost their desire to record pop music. Every so often they would find a new singer and record "the next big thing." But King Records was destined to remain a roots music label, which was not bad. At least it had found its niche in the competitive record industry. (Author's collection.)

Six

DADDY-O DAYS

By 1955, Bonnie Lou needed another hit. So King Records experimented. Louis Innis, King Records' A and R man from Indiana, wrote a song called "Daddy-O" with singer Charlie Gore and musician Buford Abner. It was cutting-edge rockabilly—teenage fare. And it hit big. (Author's collection.)

King Records signed Texan Trini Lopez in 1957, hoping to make him the Hispanic Elvis—or at least another Carl Perkins. In Dallas in 1958, Lopez recorded a couple of singles, but they did not sell nationally. This was still a year before another young Hispanic, Ritchie Valens, arrived on the national charts with Del-Fi Records of California. (Author's collection.)

In early 1959, Lopez came to King's Cincinnati studio to record "Rock On" and three other songs. Although the company tried hard to promote them, the timing was not yet right. Lopez would have to modify his musical style and wait until 1963 to start a five-year run on the singles charts that began with "If I Had a Hammer" on Reprise Records. (Author's collection.)

Vol. 1

THE TEENAGE IDOL

TRINI LOPEZ

-Side A-
"JEANIE MARIE" 2:10
"IT SEEMS" 2:30

-Side B-
"DON'T GO" 2:14
"LOVE ME TONIGHT" 2:58

JUKE BOX SPECIAL

Billy "Crash" Craddock, a North Carolina rockabilly and country singer, came to King Records in 1964. In the Cincinnati studio he recorded "Teardrops on Your Letter" and other singles but with little success. In 1969, he found his first elusive hit with "Knock Three Times" on Nashville's Cartwheel Records. He earned his nickname by crashing through opposing football teams' lines in high school. (Author's collection.)

Lattie Moore of Indianapolis was a country singer when he recorded for King Records, but in the late 1950s he was recording some rockabilly-tinged songs for independent labels. In 1963, he came to Cincinnati to record "Honky Tonk Heaven" backed with "Just About Then." He kept this photograph in a drawer for years without looking at it. (Author's collection.)

Kentucky native Ray "Orangie" Hubbard worked in a Cincinnati automobile factory by day and played music by night. In the 1950s, the singer-songwriter recorded hot rockabilly for El Rader's Lucky Records and other small Cincinnati labels, and by the mid-1960s he was recording for King Records. (Courtesy of Ray Hubbard.)

The company issued singles such as "Peepin' Tom," and Hubbard was hopeful. "But then Syd Nathan died," he said. "That left me in limbo." He continued to perform in nightclubs around town and gained a reputation as a country and rockabilly original. "When I joined King," he remembered, "Mr. Nathan said, 'Look, boy, you ain't the best damn singer I ever heard, but you're not the worst. Here's a contract. Make up your mind.'" (Courtesy of Ray Hubbard.)

Ray Pennington performed in Cincinnati-area clubs with his large country band. By 1961, he started working as a clerk at King Records, and soon he was promoted to A and R man. His own releases were under Ray Pennington or the pseudonym Ray Starr. He said he tried to record country as Ray Pennington and rock 'n' roll as Ray Starr, but the styles were interchangeable. His band backed other King Records acts on sessions, including Swanee Caldwell. Pennington also produced the Stanley Brothers and Hawkshaw Hawkins's 1963 comeback hit "Lonesome 7-7203." He said, "We'll never see another record company like King again. Syd Nathan was a genius. If he couldn't find the singer he wanted, he'd buy somebody's [old] masters. That's how he got Patsy Cline, I believe." (Author's collection.)

Al Henderson once performed with King Records' rockabilly band Boyd Bennett and His Rockets. In 1962, he recorded a solo single that was more company promotion than commercial record. "Lemon Twist" was another variation of the popular twist and a type of ice cream from All Star Dairies. Unlike most King Records releases, the single was orange and labeled first edition. (Author's collection.)

Dale Wright, a Middletown native who recorded in the King Records studio for Fraternity Records, once said this photograph shows his old band, the Rock-Its, rehearsing in the King Recording Studio for a session around 1956. There Wright recorded "She's Neat" for Fraternity Records. His later group was Dale Wright and the Wright Guys. (Courtesy of Dale Wright.)

94

Charlie Ryan's rockabilly songs "Hot Rod Lincoln" and "Side Car Saddle" arrived on the country and pop charts in 1960. They were released on the independent 4 Star Records of California, but King Records distributed the label. King issued Ryan's subsequent LP, which came at the end of the rockabilly craze. "It was nice while it lasted," Ryan said. (Author's collection.)

This photograph shows Rusty York (center) with guitarist Hap Arnold (left) and drummer Rick Sticks (right). "A guy from King called me and said, 'Can you sing like Buddy Holly?' I said, 'Oh, sure.' But I had no idea." As a result, York covered "Peggy Sue" for King in 1957. In 1961, he cut more King Records rockabilly in "Tore Up Over You" and "Love Struck." (Courtesy of Rusty York.)

SEVENTEEN

Words and Music by JOHN F. YOUNG, Jr., CHUCK GORMAN and BOYD BENNETT

As Recorded by
BOYD BENNETT AND HIS ROCKETS
on King Record No. 1470

Boyd Bennett and His Rockets exploded with the rockabilly hit "Seventeen" in 1955. He cowrote the song after a colleague at a Louisville television station talked about his 17-year-old daughter. Through 1956, King also issued two other less successful hits by the group, "My Boy—Flat Top" and "Blue Suede Shoes." But King failed to adapt to the sounds of a fast-changing rock 'n' roll scene. (Author's collection.)

DADDY-O

Words and Music by BUFORD ABNER, CHARLIE GORE and LOUIS INNIS
AS RECORDED BY BONNIE LOU FOR KING RECORDS

BONNIE LOU

MAR-KAY PUBLISHING CO.
Sole Selling Agent: KEYS MUSIC, INC.   146 West 54th Street, New York 19, N. Y.

Although "Daddy-O" was a national rockabilly hit in 1955, there was a problem—Bonnie was not happy. She considered herself country and so did her audience on WLW-T. Then the station rejected her request for time off to tour and her follow-up singles—some cut in New York—flopped. From July to November 1955, though, King Records rocked the airwaves with "Daddy-O" and "Seventeen." (Author's collection.)

Although Bennett's "Seventeen" sounds hopelessly old fashioned today, in 1955 it was hip, young music. Bennett, a native of Muscle Shoals, Alabama, remained with King Records for a few years before moving on to Mercury Records in 1959, where he had a small chart record called "Boogie Bear." But even then, rock music had started grooming smoother singers such as Frankie Avalon. In only four years, the evolving rock 'n' roll sound had grown far beyond Bennett's upright bass and country feel. Compared with the new rock acts (no more rockabilly for them), Bennett already seemed a musical dinosaur. His King Records single "Hit That Jive, Jack" sounded like music from another world. Bennett's band recorded most of its music in King's Cincinnati studio, which limited the Rockets' exposure to the burgeoning rock scene in New York. Because King's strength was in country and blues, company executives did not foresee the rapid changes that were coming in rock 'n' roll. Consequently, Bennett failed to adapt. (Author's collection.)

In 1954, Charlie Feathers started recording for Sun Records in Memphis. But King Records wanted him to help fill out a small but expanding rockabilly roster that was inspired by the success of Elvis Presley. Feathers did not make any hits for King Records, but he did record some now highly collectable singles including "Bottle to the Baby." (Courtesy of Charlie Feathers.)

King Records signed Wesley Erwin "Mac" Curtis (center) while he was in high school. A principal actually came to his classroom to tell him personally that a King Records producer wanted him to record that night in Dallas. "They thought I could be their Elvis," he said. Mac performed with Alan Freed's rock shows in New York in 1956. Later he went country and worked in radio. (Courtesy of Mac Curtis.)

Seven

ROYALTY

This portrait photograph shows Sydney Nathan, founder of King Records, as he appeared when his company was starting to break big nationally, around 1946. Note that he is not wearing the heavy black glasses that he wore later in life. (Courtesy of Zella Nathan.)

Syd Nathan and Henry Glover (left), King Records' chief A and R man for rhythm and blues, congratulate staff member and vibes player Gene Redd (right), who worked for the company for years as a staff musician, recording artist, and producer. After leaving King Records in the 1960s, Redd discovered Kool and the Gang. (Courtesy of Steven D. Halper.)

Making a record deal? Nathan poses with unidentified men in his office at 1540 Brewster Avenue, where he conducted business for a quarter century. This photograph, from around 1960, was printed directly from a large color negative owned by his wife. King advisor Joe Thomas is on the far right. (Courtesy of Zella Nathan.)

As usual, Nathan looks dapper and ready for business in this c. 1957 photograph. He once told members of his A and R staff that one perk of working for King Records was that they could afford attractive clothes. He wore colorful ties and smoked big cigars. His tie is monogrammed "SN." (Courtesy of Steven D. Halper.)

In his office around 1966, Nathan prepares to listen to a vinyl record while holding his little dog. He was there for an interview with a newspaper reporter. Local newspapers did not give King much publicity, considering its major achievements, but at times the stories were detailed. He framed one longer *Cincinnati Enquirer* story and hung it on the wall behind his desk. (Courtesy of the Cincinnati Enquirer.)

This c. 1964 picture should be titled "Battle of the Missiles," considering the size of the cigars involved. But what can one expect when Syd Nathan meets arch competitor Herman Lubinsky (right), owner of Savoy Records of New Jersey, at a music awards party. The unidentified man in the middle looks as if he wants to say, "Come on, fellows, make peace for a moment." (Courtesy of Zella Nathan.)

Nathan appears at a c. 1946 country music show. With him are Homer and Jethro, kneeling, Cowboy Copas, upper right, and Grandpa Jones, upper left. The man between them appears to be Nelson King, WCKY's *Jamboree* host. Nathan sometimes attended indoor and outdoor performances with his acts. (Courtesy of Zella Nathan.)

To celebrate Nathan's 25th anniversary in the record business, friends and family celebrated with a party and printed a special tribute to him. A commemorative booklet for the event shows Nathan adorned, fittingly, with a crown. (Courtesy of Zella Nathan.)

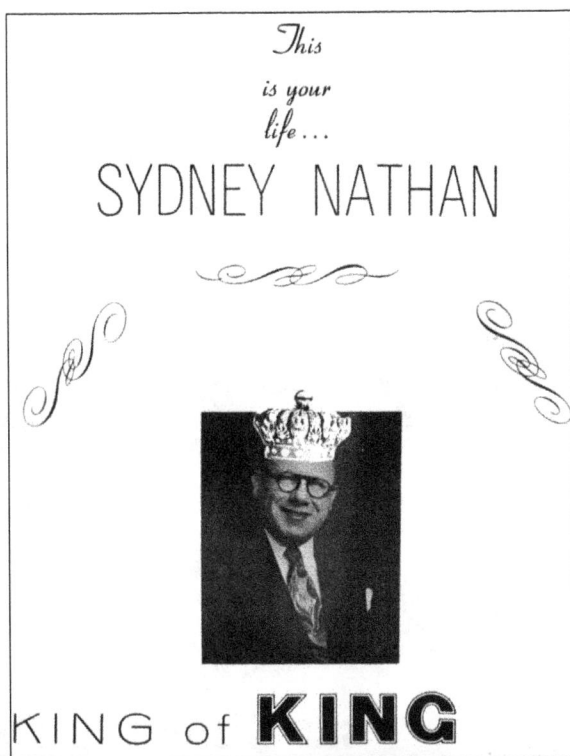

This is your life...

SYDNEY NATHAN

KING of **KING**

In this *c.* 1966 photograph, Nathan accepts a gold record for another James Brown best seller, "I Got You (I Feel Good)," which hit No. 1 on the R&B chart in November 1965. Brown's band cut it at Criteria Recording in Miami. The studio was Nathan's favorite outside of Cincinnati. (Courtesy of Zella Nathan.)

KING RECORDS

COWBOY COPAS

LONNIE JOHNSON

MOON MULLICAN

BULLMOOSE JACKSON

GRANDPA JONES

CECIL GANT

EARL BOSTIC

SEPT. 1948

HILLBILLY

NOVELTY

SEPIA

BLUES

IVORY JOE HUNTER

WYNONIE HARRIS

TODD RHODES

HANK PENNY

TEXAS RUBY

MARION ABERNATHY

CLYDE MOODY

Halpers

RECORDS BY MAIL

132 W. Fifth St. - DUnbar 6580 - Cincinnati 2, Ohio

HAWKSHAW HAWKINS

A King Records catalog from September 1948 shows some big names in country and blues. At the bottom of the brochure, Halper's Records is listed. At the time, King Records investors Saul and Dorothy Halper continued to operate their Cincinnati record shop. She was Sydney Nathan's sister. Other original backers—their investment totaled a little less than $25,000—included Howard Kessel, Nathan's second cousin, and Doris Nathan, wife of Syd's physician brother David. Syd Nathan used his limited seed money wisely when he started in late 1943. Four years later, *Billboard* and jukebox operators ranked King Records the No. 6 record company in the United States, placing it ahead of Mercury, Sonora, and others. *Billboard* commented that King Records' finish surprised people because the company was so young. But as the magazine added, King Records "literally dominates the field." (Author's collection.)

Dorothy and Saul Halper, Syd Nathan's sister and brother-in-law, pose in this 1970s photograph. She and her husband joined a small group of friends and family to invest in Nathan's dream. Through financial good times and bad, they remained partners with him until his death in 1968. (Courtesy of Steven D. Halper.)

This image is printed on the side of a box of 45-rpm singles from the mid-1960s. King Records shipped millions of records from its Royal Plastics pressing plant in Evanston. The company pressed its own records as well as custom orders for other record labels, individuals, and producers. (Author's collection.)

Syd Nathan, third from right in the second row, stands next to Henry Glover (left) and Tiny Bradshaw (right) in a gathering of music people. Howard Kessel, King executive, is first on the left in the first row. (Courtesy of Zella Nathan.)

In this c. 1966 photograph, Syd Nathan relaxes in the sun, probably in Miami Beach, where he vacationed. He often recorded at Miami's Criteria studios and modeled some of his studio equipment after Criteria's. Through the years, he was treated at the Miami Heart Institute. (Courtesy of Zella Nathan.)

Eight

MR. DYNAMITE

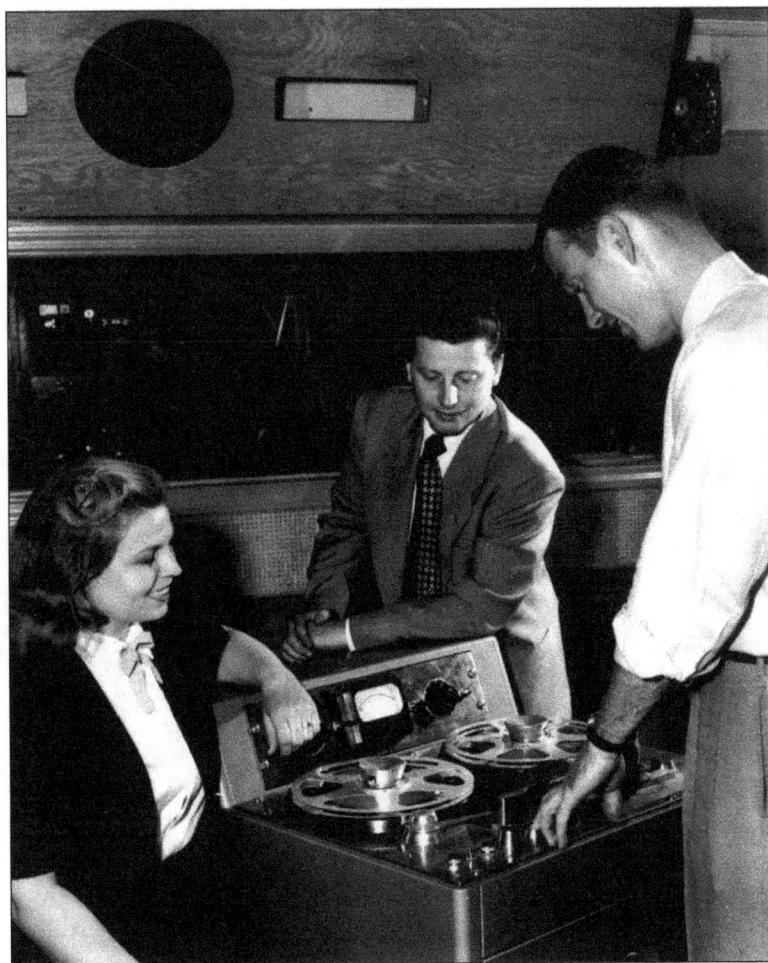

In this 1952 photograph, pop vocalist Ruby Wright discusses a monaural recording in the King Records studio with pianist-engineer Eddie Smith (center) and engineer Bob Ellis. Later, Smith left for a job at Bell Sound Studios in New York, where he engineered Dionne Warwick's "Walk on By." (Photograph by Allan Kain, courtesy of the Cincinnati Enquirer.)

This is where the real action happened in the 1940s, the offices at King Records. Note the large national map that identifies radio airplay sites from coast to coast. On the wall is a poster of country artists Homer and Jethro, whose most impressive hits would come later on RCA-Victor from 1949 to 1959. (Courtesy of Zella Nathan.)

Employees work with "mothers," metal 78-rpm record-stamping discs, in the late 1940s. After the 45-rpm single and long-playing albums were introduced in 1949, King Records' Royal Plastics division retooled to manufacture vinyl discs—seven-inch singles and extended play albums, 10-inch records, and 12-inch long-playing albums. One King Records single was called "Big Ten Inch Record." (Courtesy of Howard Kessel.)

Women employees stuff albums into paper sleeves around 1958. King Records employed many women in the plant, which became extremely hot in the summer. Despite the uncomfortable working conditions, many of the workers stayed at King Records for decades. It was a union-represented factory. (Courtesy of Steven D. Halper.)

Two artists work in the King Records art department, run by Dan Quest. He designed many of King's LP covers. Often distinctive but garish, King Records' albums stood out from the competition. Having its own art department made King unusual among independent labels. (Courtesy of Steven D. Halper.)

Bill Schultz, King Records' first real recording engineer, listens to a tape in the King Records recording studio's mastering room around 1953. After a singer or group recorded a song on tape, an engineer took it to the mastering department, which was next to the studio, to be prepared for the pressing plant. Schultz helped set up the new studio in late 1947 and early 1948. (Courtesy of Steven D. Halper.)

This is the entrance to King Records' Royal Plastics Division as it appeared around 1959. Howard Kessel, who ran the division, said King Records was selling 20,000 records a week by that time. "James Brown was keeping the company alive," he said. (Courtesy of Howard Kessel.)

This 1953 photograph shows an unidentified factory worker separating a stamper—a metal mold from which vinyl records are pressed. That year, King Records' independent union merged with the Vending Machine Service Employees Union, Local 122. *Billboard* noted that this was the first time a jukebox union had signed a contract with any record company. (Courtesy of Howard Kessel.)

HANK MARR TRIO + 3

TEENTIME *latest dance steps*
THE BOSSA NOVA · THE LIMBO · THE MADIS
THE POPEYE · SLOW DANCE · THE ROOS
THE TWIST · THE WATUSI · THE MON
THE FISH · THE STOMP · THE SWIM · THE DRI

ViViD SOUND

Hank Marr, organist, poses with sax man Rusty Bryant and drummer Taylor Orr. King groomed Marr as Bill Doggett's successor. Both recorded R&B in the 1960s. Although he was never as commercially popular as Doggett, Marr cut a number of singles and albums for the Federal subsidiary and later for King Records itself. One of his instrumentals was "Greasy Spoon." Later Marr became a music professor in Columbus. (Courtesy of David Meyers.)

This 1961 King Records trade advertisement promotes James Brown, Hank Ballard, and other R&B acts. Ballard recorded yet another dance number, "Continental Walk," while Doggett did another "Tonk" record. Apparently the advertisement copywriter was responsible for the misspelling of Doggett's song title. (Author's collection.)

Dee Felice organized the Mixed Feelings in Cincinnati around 1969. Critics compared the band with the Fifth Dimension and Blood, Sweat, and Tears. At times, the group included Frank Vincent, piano; Lee Tucker, bass; and vocalist Randy Crawford. They performed a jazz-pop sound at New York's Village Gate and appeared on television shows hosted by Steve Allen, David Frost, Joey Bishop, Merv Griffin, and Mike Douglas. (Courtesy of Shelly Nelson.)

Syd Nathan opened his own pressing plant in November 1944, citing the unreliability of many independent plants. By using his own presses, Nathan could manufacture as few or as many discs as needed—at considerably less cost per unit. Most independents did not own their own presses. They were too expensive to maintain and operate. (Courtesy of Steven D. Halper.)

This photograph shows women working in the King pressing plant around 1955. "We used to grind up our old records and melt them down to recycle the vinyl," said Howard Kessel, president of Royal Plastics. "We didn't want to waste anything." Often the plant ran on two shifts. (Courtesy of Steven D. Halper.)

Saucy comedian Ruth Wallis of Brooklyn came to King Records when Syd Nathan acquired DeLuxe Records in the late 1940s. For years, she continued to record for King Records' DeLuxe subsidiary, and later King issued her material on albums under its logo. Wallis sang in lounges, where her double entendre humor became popular. Blonde and blustery, she successfully filled a niche occupied by only a few women comics. King Records described her style as "adult humor for humorous adults" and "risqué all the way." Her records—the equivalent of brief nightclub monologues—were intended for parties, not radio. Compared with today's rough material, however, her songs almost seem tame. During a long career, she also recorded for Mercury, Monarch, and other companies. She retired in the 1970s, just in time to avoid the onslaught of modern raunchy humor. (Author's collection.)

E

IEST

CORDED

UND

IG RECORDING STUDIO

1540 BREWSTER AVE.
CINCINNATI 7, OHIO

PL. 1-2211

RATE SCHEDULE

KING RECORDING STUDIO

PLaza 1-2211

The King Records recording studio operated at 1540 Brewster Avenue from October 1947 through the end of 1971. In 1949, Nathan and A and R man Henry Glover, a trumpet player from Lucky Millinder's band, built the original echo chamber—one of the earliest of such devices. Although normally the studio was not equipped with the latest equipment, it did offer an excellent sound. Hundreds of national and regional hits came from it, including James Brown's "Cold Sweat" and "Mother Popcorn" in the 1960s. Little Willie John recorded "Fever" there on March 1, 1955. The Casinos came to King Records to record "Then You Can Tell Me Goodbye" on four tracks. Independent producers, including Herman Griffin, also rented the studio, and subsequently sold their masters to national labels. (Courtesy of Steven D. Halper.)

This trade advertisement, from around 1951, offers the services of King Records' pressing plant, Royal Plastics. It operated from late 1944 until late 1971, when parent label Starday Records closed it. Plastics chief Howard Kessel once admitted that King Records' pressings were competent but not always up to expectations. The author found this out in 1970, when an independent record label pressed his first record at King Records. (Author's collection.)

The Dolphins sing in the King Studio during the 1964 session that yielded "Hey-Da-Da-Dow" for Fraternity Records. Not shown is recording engineer Dave Harrison. The band consisted of guitarist and songwriter Carl Edmondson (center) and vocalists Marv Lockwood (left) and Paul Singleton (right). Edmondson frequently used the studio, creating the hits "Memphis" and "Wham!" by Lonnie Mack there. (Courtesy of Carl Edmondson.)

THE DEE FELICE QUARTET

KENNY POOLE...Guitar   **DEE FELICE...Drums**

In 1968, Bethlehem, primarily a jazz imprint, released an instrumental single of Jim Webb's "Wichita Lineman" by the talented Dee Felice Trio. The Cincinnati-based group added guitarist Kenny Poole and evolved into a quartet, pictured above. Felice played drums; Frank Vincent, piano; and Lee Tucker, electric bass. At times, the musicians worked as King Records studio session men, providing music for James Brown and other acts. They shared credits with him on album cuts that year. In the Cincinnati studio in 1970, Vincent and Poole played on Brown's "Georgia on My Mind," and the year before Poole played on parts one and two of "Mother Popcorn." (Above courtesy of Shelly Nelson; right, author's collection.)

117

In 1962, before the "English Invasion" changed American radio, King Records signed the Impacs, a clean-cut rock band. They recorded singles and an album, mainly in Miami. They enjoyed playing surfing music. But their records did not perform sufficiently to dent the increasingly competitive pop charts. (Author's collection.)

Before he transformed himself into a sitcom star in the 1970s, Redd Foxx recorded comedy albums for independent record companies, including King Records in the late 1960s. One such album featured a color photograph of Foxx with an arm wrapped around a young woman. They were both nude—but shot from the rear. (Author's collection.)

In the late 1940s, King Records started issuing press releases about its artists and published a company newsletter called *Platter Patter*. Another regular publication, which provided company news to workers, was a bulletin called *King Komments*. (Author's collection.)

Platter Patter
PUBLISHED FOR AND BY KING RECORD EMPLOYEES

Vol. I   October, 1947   No. 5

KING, UNION REACH AGREEMENT FOR
COMING YEAR

EXPANSION OF KING FACILITIES, OFFICE SPACE MOVING FORWARD

The clatter of hammers and the smell of fresh paint are familiar to King employees who have had a chance to travel around the plant in the past few weeks. In various parts of the buildings, construction of additional space for expanding departments is going ahead.

Perhaps by the time this issue of Platter Patter is in your hands, members of the addressograph and file sections may have moved into their new quarters adjoining the bookkeeping department and up over the shipping room.

WATCH KING'S PROGRESS

This move will give the two sections room that they have long been seeking and, in addition, will enable Bill Schultz to have more room for his new recording studio.

By spring, the new quarters will be refinished and decorated in keeping with the style in the bookkeeping and accounting office.

Other changes slated for completion in the near future involve the installation of steel shelving in the Shipping Department so that the shipping clerks will be able to reach the record stocks without trudging miles and miles each day.

Workers in the Inspection Department
(Continued on page 4)

Officials of the King Record Distributing Co. and the Federation of Record Manufactuer's Employees Union have signed a new contract replacing one which expired Friday, Sept. 12th. The new agreement will be valid until Sept. 1, 1948.

LABOR
MANAGEMENT

Negotiations had been going on for several weeks between the officers of the two groups and a series of discussions were climaxed with the signing of a new contract on Friday, Sept. 26. Terms of the agreement are retroactive to September 12.

In the main, the new contract is similar to the old one but there are several new features. Several of the wage rates have been raised in some of the departments, notably, the mill room, inspection and testing, and in shipping.

A second major change is the new provision which will enable employees to earn up to two weeks vacation per year. Details of the plan will be made known in a short time. Office employees of KING, not covered by the union contract, may also be able to earn the same vacation privileges, but the details have not been worked out.

Copies of the new contract will be printed and made available in the near future.

For Immediate Release!
News FROM KING RECORDS
1540 BREWSTER AVE., CINCINNATI 7, OHIO

RELEASE ON RECEIPT

For its first release in 1948, King Records has chosen a group of tunes by some of its top artists for distribution in January. These are the first in a group to be released this year and despite the Petrillo ban, King will be able to supply more top tunes on both its Red and Blue label throughout the year.

Heading the list of Red Label records is the second release by Jack Perry and the Lightcrust Doughboys on the King label. One of the most popular novelty tunes, "The Sow Song" is given a new treatment by the Doughboys on King 687. The tune is backed by the "Fisherman's Polka". The Doughboys, widely-known south-western vocal and instrumental group, work out of Fort Worth, Texas and Station W B A P. In addition to their King recording activities, the boys have several radio shows each week over WBAP and stations of the Texas Quality Network. The boys were organized some years ago by Sen. W. Lee O'Daniel in his campaign for the Texas governorship. O'Daniel, then a flour manufacturer, gave the group their name after one of his products.

Another one of the Delmore Brother's famous boogie tunes is scheduled for release by King. On the King Red Label # 680, the boys have waxed "Mobile Boogie", backed by "Waitin' For That Train". The Delmore have been kept busy during the past months with programs over WMC in

-----more

At its peak in those days, the company employed a staff of two public relations officers. (Author's collection.)

119

The Billboard 1954 Disk Jockey Poll

R & B FAVORITES...

Instrumental
GROUPS OR BANDS

Based on actual vote of disk jockeys covering period of January 1, 1954, thru October 9, 1954.

Which are your favorite Rhythm and Blues instrumental groups or bands!

PLACE	WINNER	LABEL
1.	EARL BOSTIC	King
2.	TINY BRADSHAW	King
3.	BILL DOGGETT	King
4.	ARNETT COBB	Atlantic
5.	BUDDY JOHNSON	Mercury
6.	TAB SMITH	United
7.	FATS DOMINO	Imperial
8.	BIG JAY McNEELY	Federal
9.	COUNT BASIE	Clef
10.	DUKE ELLINGTON	Capitol
11.	JOE LOCO	Tico
12.	RUSTY BRYANT	Dot
13.	GRIFFIN BROTHERS	Dot

"CREAM OF THE CROP..."

4 OUT OF THE TOP 6!

PHONE • WRITE • WIRE **UNIVERSAL ATTRACTIONS**
2 PARK AVENUE • NEW YORK 16, N. Y.

Universal Attractions, a New York booking agency, distributed this poster in 1954. It touted the most popular black American instrumentalists according to demand for their concerts. Interestingly five of the top eight had recorded for or still did record for King Records and its family of labels. Those performers were Tiny Bradshaw, Bill Doggett, Big Jay McNeely, Tab Smith, and Earl Bostic. Although tenor sax man McNeely never had a hit on King Records' Federal label (he had hit earlier for arch competitor Savoy), he did record an instrumental for Federal called "Nervous Man Nervous." It could have been the independent label owner's theme song. (Author's collection.)

James Brown came to Cincinnati to record himself and other acts, search for talent, and relax. He could be seen browsing in Dino's downtown clothing store, where he bought dozens of suits. The store thanked him in this 1971 trade advertisement, prompted by then–King Records owner Hal Neely's sale of Brown's contract to Polydor Records of New York. (Author's collection.)

We at Dino's are proud to have played a large part in creating the fashion image of the legendary James Brown. We happily join with Billboard, Cincinnati and the world in honoring a true humanitarian.

Dino's 16 EAST SIXTH STREET • CINCINNATI, OHIO 45202

After Syd Nathan's death in 1968, King Records went through several ownership changes. This logo—the label's third major one—appeared in 1972, when producer-writers Jerry Leiber and Mike Stoller produced in New York and partner Hal Neely administered the company from Nashville. Their first act was an older one, the Coasters. Soon Neely would sell his stake to his partners on a coin toss and regret it. (Author's collection.)

121

This advertisement promotes James Brown as *Record World*'s No. 1 male R&B vocalist for 1969. By then, he was recording for Starday-King, after the two companies had merged. He cut the hit single "Let a Man Come In and Do the Popcorn" in the Cincinnati studio, which Starday-King continued to operate until 1971. At that time, the company removed much of the recording equipment and the instruments—including the Hammond B3 organ used by James Brown—to the Starday Records studio in suburban Nashville. (Author's collection.)

the now sound of
WAYNE COCHRAN
and his C.C. RIDERS

Vocal
"IF I WERE A CARPENTER"
King #6288

Instrumental
"HEY JUDE—ELEANOR RIGBY"
Bethlehem #3097

STARDAY ✱ KING
recording and publishing companies inc.

Like matter and antimatter, there had to be a white aspirant to King Records' title of Mr. Dynamite. He was Wayne Cochran, complete with bleached pompadour and more moves than a gyroscope. He too recorded for King Records in 1969, releasing albums and singles. Once his large horn band, the C. C. Riders, competed against Brown's (minus James) group in a showdown at a Dayton club. Starday must have really liked Cochran, for it simultaneously released two different records on two of its labels—"If I Were a Carpenter," his remake of the Bobby Darin hit, on King Records, as well as his band's medley instrumental, "Hey Jude–Eleanor Rigby," on Bethlehem. Both were recorded in Cincinnati. Earlier in his career, Cochran recorded for various companies and wrote "Last Kiss" by J. Frank Wilson and the Cavaliers. (Author's collection.)

Another nickname that James Brown received from his label was Mr. Dynamite. And dynamite he was, exploding on stage with all the energy of five men. He earned the title of the hardest-working man in show business. In 1968 and 1969, he often recorded in King Records' Cincinnati studio and operated his independent production company in the Brewster Avenue building. He recorded Kay Robinson, the Dapps, Marva Whitney, Vickie Anderson, and other performers. (Author's collection.)

25

★ YEARS ★

AS

KING of **KING**

From Memory Lane

HAWKSHAW HAWKINS   COWBOY COPAS   MOON MULLICAN

When a tribute party was held shortly before Syd Nathan's death, he was crowned the king of King. He ruled his empire like a king, for only he knew what he wanted to hear. Some of his artists were pictured on the night's program. (Courtesy of Zella Nathan.)

In better times, Syd Nathan laughs and plays the drums in a restaurant. Through the decades, his own beat goes on in the hundreds of King Records recordings that he produced from 1943 to 1968. He is the father of the modern independent record company concept and an able steward of American roots music. (Courtesy of Steven D. Halper.)

BIBLIOGRAPHY

Brown, James, and Bruce Tucker. *James Brown: The Godfather of Soul*. New York: Macmillan, 1986.

Dawson, Jim, and Steve Propes. *What Was the First Rock 'n' Roll Record?* Boston: Faber and Faber, 1992.

———. *45 RPM: The History, Heroes & Villains of a Pop Music Revolution*. San Francisco: Backbeat Books, 2003.

Gentry, Linnell. *A History and Encyclopedia of Country, Western, and Gospel Music*. Nashville, TN: Clairmont Corporation, 1969.

Kennedy, Rick, and Randy McNutt. *Little Labels—Big Sound: Small Record Companies and the Rise of American Music*. Bloomington, IN: Indiana University Press, 1999.

McNutt, Randy. *Guitar Towns: A Journey to the Crossroads of Rock 'n' Roll*. Bloomington, IN: Indiana University Press, 2002.

———. *We Wanna Boogie: An Illustrated History of the American Rockabilly Movement*. Hamilton, OH: HHP Books, 1989.

Ruppli, Michel. *The King Labels: A Discography*. Westport, CT: Greenwood Press, 1985.

Whitburn, Joel. *Top Pop, 1955–1982*. Menomonee Falls, WI: Record Research, 1983.

———. *Top Country Singles, 1944–1988*. Menomonee Falls, WI: Record Research, 1988.

———. *Top R&B Singles, 1942–1988*. Menomonee Falls, WI: Record Research, 1988.

Visit us at
arcadiapublishing.com

www.ingramcontent.com/pod-product-compliance
Lightning Source LLC
Chambersburg PA
CBHW050643110426
42813CB00007B/1895